Set in the author's ho.

ing story of Leonor, former child soldier of the FARC, a rural guerrilla group.

Paula Delgado-Kling followed Leonor for nineteen years, from shortly after she was an active member of the FARC forced into sexual slavery by a commander thirty-four years her senior, through her rehabilitation and struggle with alcohol and drug addiction, to more recent days as the mother of two girls.

Leonor's physical beauty, together with resourcefulness and imagination in the face of horrendous circumstances, helped her carve a space for herself in a male-dominated world. She never stopped believing that she was a woman of worth and importance. It took her many years of therapy to accept that she was also a victim.

Throughout the story of *Leonor*, Delgado-Kling interweaves the experiences of her own family, involved with Colombian politics since the nineteenth century and deeply afflicted, too, by the decades of violence there.

LEONOR

Leonor

The Story of a Lost Childhood

PAULA DELGADO-KLING

Evergreen Review Books

Published by Evergreen Review Books, an imprint of OR Books

Visit our website at www.evergreenreview.com

All rights information: rights@orbooks.com

First printing 2024

Cataloging-in-Publication data is available from the Library of Congress. A catalog record for this book is available from the British Library.

paperback ISBN 978-1-68219-447-8 • ebook ISBN 978-1-68219-448-5

Cover art: "Massacre of two paramilitaries" by "Marta" (former combatant, Revolutionary Armed Forces of Colombia, FARC-EP), 2009. Courtesy Fundación Puntos de Encuentro. Design by Pocomeloso.

For Leonor

Préstame tu lanza lancero, que siento ganas de pelear,
cuando se levante mi pueblo, al yanqui vamos a acabar.
A pelear llama este acordéon, vamos pueblo para la trinchera,
porque para el rico ladrón, hay pertecho en la cartuchera.

Lend me your lance, lancer, I feel like fighting,
when my people rise, we will end the Yankee.
This accordion calls to fight, let's go, people, to the trench,
because for the rich thief, there is ammunition in
the holster.

—FARC song

"I write entirely to find out what I'm thinking, what I'm
looking at, what I see and what it means. What I want and
what I fear."

—Joan Didion

A NOTE FROM THE AUTHOR

This is a work of nonfiction. For many years, Leonor patiently reconstructed for me painful episodes of her life, but most occurred when she was a child under immense stress, and memory can be flawed. I have tried to be accurate and loyal to her story. I have wherever possible provided sources to corroborate the narrative, which can be found as endnotes in the back of the book. Some of the people in this book, though not all, requested pseudonyms—including Leonor. Public figures are identified by their real names.

INTRODUCTION

I stayed weekends in La Sabana, Bogotá's countryside, with my grandmother. Helena was already a widow by then, and she lived alone in a house in northern Bogotá—a grand house, with a Rodin and a Botero in the foyer, and Chagalls and Picassos in the salon. But I had no sense of the artists' genius, not until it was too late to ask my grandmother what drew her to their work. What mattered then was to get out and explore atop my ten-speed bike under the blue sky. I rode past the gardeners, away from the gate and the evergreen bushes that guarded the grounds, and onto the cow pastures on the other side.

I was my happiest outdoors, and had no thoughts of danger or kidnappings. Under the early morning fog, the Holsteins lowed, their echo like the notes of a saxophone, and the calves answered like playful little trumpets, their muzzles peeping out from under the overgrown grass. At midday, the sun broiled the air, and the clouds hung low. Around us were mountain chains, and the sky's reflection painted them a light shade of blue or grey. Once the fog lifted, majestic pine and eucalyptus trees appeared, and they lined gravel paths leading to the cattle's milking stations and to the barn. Along these paths, I pedaled the bike—as fast as only an eight-year-old can, cutting corners, taking flight on each bump, nudging it up a gear—and the eucalyptus branches swayed like fans on the stands, arms raised. The joy! All species of birds—cardinals, parakeets, hummingbirds, swallows—attended to their chit-chat. Some flew to the kitchen window and immersed themselves in conversation with the canaries inside the hanging cages. The canaries—nurtured by Don Leo—were transplants from the warmer weather, a three-hour drive away, at my grandmother's pool house, named California, and overseen by Don Leo and his wife, Doña Margarita. They were beloved by our family. They sent me sticks of sugarcane to gnaw on.

I rode the bike right up to the shores of the Bogotá River where there were three or four hive stands, and adults shouted out to beware the sting of the bees. By the afternoon, the caretaker's long stick queued the cattle for the last milking of the day. The breeze dispersed a heavy floral scent. It was like dipping your face in rosewater. It came from the greenhouses on a neighboring property, in the distance seen only as white dots, where rows of roses, carnations, and alstroemerias grew for export. During the few minutes before sundown, you felt swaddled inside a papaya, such was the color all around.

I took off my shoes when entering the house. (That was a rule. There was wall-to-wall white carpeting.) Meals with my grandmother were served on sparkling silver dishes. Curried chicken and papadums, coquilles Saint Jacques, pepper soup, the kinds of platters you would expect if she was hosting a party. Doña Helena doesn't eat regular food, the cook told me.

At bedtime, I heard the ice in my grandmother's whiskey clank inside the glass. Life with my grandfather, Fernando, had conditioned her to follow politics—he was mayor of Bogotá four times—and she stayed up until the end of the nine o'clock news.

Those weekends, she talked a lot about my grandfather. Helena told me (another ice cube melting, another drink to pass time, and I sensed my mother had sent me to keep her company) that it had been Fernando's plan to buy land outside Bogotá and to rent it out to cattle growers, and to wait until our capital city expanded, until there was a market demand to turn the property into suburban housing. What might he think that for three generations now—my father took over from him, and now my older brother was the boss—our family's business involved transforming the pastures he left us into paved streets and neighborhoods with stop signs and traffic lights. Would Fernando say that the men in our family had honored his vision?

It took them patience and perseverance to get the work done. The acquiring of permits from the city, the politics with different municipal administrations, the negotiations with the electric and aqueduct companies, and finally, the magic of turning bricks into homes. Clumps of the native pine and eucalyptus trees stood out among rooftops, and their broad roots tore up the grounds of public parks. Schools, gyms, supermarkets, car dealerships, two country clubs, a Kumon learning center, and malls with H&M and Zara brought traffic jams and road rage.

Not far from where the hive stands once stood, on the opposite shore of the Bogotá River, an anti-narcotics military base was set up in recent years. The comings and goings of the army's choppers caused our windows and chandeliers to wobble. At all hours, day and night, the turbulent sound injected itself, into golf games, tennis matches, garden parties, and it served as an alarm—listen up! Horrors have been occurring, for decades now. Pay attention to the suffering of our fellow countrymen.

In the 1980s, the violence morphed from the countryside to the cities. This was years after my grandfather's death—long after Fernando spoke on the main square to his masses of supporters (he veered towards populist liberalism), sometime after he founded Colombia's first airline, and not so long after his construction business completed several developments. It turned out that his fame endured—a school, a stadium, and even a main thoroughfare were named after him—and it translated into my family becoming a target of kidnappings. So one day in 1984, when I was eight years old, my father said we had to leave the country. A week later, we had moved to Toronto, Canada.

There was no pressing reason for me to return to Bogotá. Once when I was a teenager, I expressed interest in the family business—probably pride as well—but my enthusiasm was squelched. I understood, in the ways that girls do, from subtle messages. Perhaps I noted the adults' choice of words, perhaps I observed the fact that only men held office jobs, definitely I took in the ways my father groomed my brother for his tenure—that because I was born a woman, my life was not to go in that direction, in the route of preserving Fernando's business legacy. Instead, my parents thought that I would marry well and be satisfied taking care of the home. It would be my duty to assure that the housekeeper polished the silver, and that she properly starched my husband's shirts and the dinner napkins, and maybe I would tend to a charity. My attention might be focused in finding recipes for coq au vin and beef bourguignon. I would be a good host, and a social being. That was their order of things. I escaped, to live abroad.

Abroad, I found greater freedom to build my life on my terms. It was exciting to allow my identity to bloom. I was an athlete. I was a volunteer in a women's shelter for victims of domestic abuse. I was a scholar.

During my graduate studies at Columbia University in New York, I heard academics and policy experts say that Colombia was not viable, it was a geopolitical risk, it was a failed state. What did they mean? They said women were the silent victims—how so? In 2001, I went back to Bogotá to collect testimonies on human rights and women's lives. There, I met Leonor, then seventeen years old. We met merely twenty days after her departure from the Revolutionary Armed Forces of Colombia, the FARC, once a deadly cocaine-trafficking group on the US State Department's terrorism list. The FARC controlled the region in southern Colombia where Leonor was born, and from a young age, she joined the group, out of the necessity to survive.

Her parents were farmers displaced by violence, low-skilled and unemployed, and preoccupied with day-to-day subsistence. They had multiple children. There were hardly any schools nearby for Leonor and her siblings to attend. The few schools that did exist were fertile recruiting ground for the FARC.

Leonor experienced domestic violence in her childhood home, and the situation led her to spend weeks, maybe months (she was unaware of time) alone on the streets. Then, in the FARC—while she was still a child—she witnessed the group's inner extrajudicial killings. She endured weeks-long battles against the government's elite soldiers. Drug trafficking was all around her.

To survive, Leonor numbed her feelings. When we first met, she had a kind of amnesia from stress, and she could not subjectively recall entire episodes of her life. For her, what had happened when and where was a puzzle. As a former FARC, the government provided her with therapy. In government therapy lingo, it was said she was "demobilizing"—which I took to mean she was examining what events, in particular, had led her to partake in a terrorist group. Slowly she was shedding the negative ways, habits, and influences she had known throughout her life. She was deciding for herself what pieces of her family and her community fit within her life.

For twenty years now, I have witnessed how she did it. She rose up, and as result of sheer will, she carved another path for herself and her two daughters. It was admirable.

All through these years, she has told me about her life, a little at a time, as she pieced back her memory. In 2001, when she was seventeen years old, she said she had joined the FARC six months earlier. In 2013, she clarified: she joined the FARC, formally at least, when she was eleven or twelve years old, and she remained in their ranks for five or six years.

As a way of an apology, Leonor said, "When you leave the guerrilla, your mind has been worked on, so you say, sort of, what seems convenient. You asked me things, I said '*aaha*, sí,' but also because I didn't know exact answers."

It was easier for her to regard the five or six years in the FARC as a mere six months. As others in her group were captured or they left the FARC voluntarily, they had photos of her. Authorities interrogated her, and when they showed her the images, she recalled events, and she was able to put her memories into context.

She mocked me. "I ask you—how can I be the commander's wife in such short time if I was there for only six months?"

At our first meetings, Leonor talked unrelentingly about Commander Tico to highlight her standing as Tico's "compañera."

She confided, "I still think of Tico all the time. Me and Tico, ours is a love story."

She planned to marry Tico atop a mountain. "Everyone will still wear the FARC uniform," Leonor explained, "and I will have an immensely long white veil.[1] And a bouquet, and the wind will blow my veil."

"That sounds romantic," I humored her. In the FARC, there were no weddings. There were casual unions in which a couple was obliged to ask the commander for permission to have sex.[2] Tico—the commander, the adult, the male, the leader—controlled the underage girls in his squad, and he did with them as he pleased.

"Sometimes, I think of going back to Tico, even now. But I can't go back there, they would kill me." After a moment, she added, "Do you think Tico would ever come here to Bogotá to fetch me?"

She was kidding herself. She fantasized the role she played in the commander's life.

The idea that she was the commander's trophy girl was a veil she invented to cover the power dynamic that men exercise over women in the FARC.[3] For years, and even into middle age, Leonor's identity stemmed from her standing as Commander Tico's top girl. He was middle-ranked and powerful. He was thirty-four years her senior.

Though our country's past might have foretold that two women from opposing worlds might never cross paths, we built our kinship over phone, e-mail, even Facebook. I found myself wanting to return to Colombia to hear the latest in her recovery. What Leonor had lived through, and what still lay ahead for her to surpass, knocked the wind out of me. Hers was the story of Colombia, and the challenges it faced.

The first time I had given thought to children using guns was days after my brother, Alejandro, was released from a kidnapping. Our family had flown to London. In the hotel suite, I overheard Alejandro speaking long distance on the telephone to his best friend in Bogotá. Alejandro thought I was in the shower and he was alone.

"They were boys, the ones who held me hostage," he was saying.

I let the water run in the shower. I returned to eavesdrop from behind the doorway.

"Fourteen year olds, probably," he said.

The floor creaked, and I fled to the bathroom.

This snippet of information was of great value to me, because my mother had forbidden me from asking Alejandro anything related to the kidnapping. It brought my parents too much pain to face it, and they referred to it as his "absence." Years later, at the end of a yoga class, in shavasana, I realized that I had gone looking for Leonor to hear her accounts firsthand, because of what I overheard in the hotel suite in London. Leonor was, in my mind, a stand-in for my brother's captors.

Understanding that, I felt half mad with clarity, and I had trouble breathing. In the ensuing days, fatigue overcame me.

At first, Leonor had not known what to make of me. She hesitated to trust me, of course, having been taught to question motives always. She was also brainwashed into maintaining utmost secrecy about her life.

I told her I was a journalist, but the idea of journalism was hard for her to understand. The fact that I lived outside Colombia—and in the US, among "imperialist Yankees," as expressed in FARC lingo—confused her further. She was taught that FARC commanders, who had been extradited to the US and convicted of drug trafficking, were "prisoners of the empire."

Nearly a decade after our first meeting, when we spoke on the telephone, she said, "I think I assumed you were a social worker. But you were nosy, so a few of us said you were a spy." Again, she giggled.

A spy for whom?

"The enemy."

What enemy?

"The government."

I reminded her that for years she had lived in halfway homes, paid for and run by the government. Her status as "demobilized," as "reinsertada," granted her that privilege.

I said, "The government even hired nutritionists for all of you."

Yet I could see why she placed me, a white, blue-eyed woman with an accent from Bogotá, as the enemy. The great divide between rural and urban Colombians resulted in distrust from the time our country was part of Spain. With further giggles, which I took as her peace offering, she confessed that at first, she wove her tales to say enough to keep my interest, while never revealing the entire truth.

I was grateful Leonor talked to me; other girls in the government homes held their fists seemingly ready to fight. But somehow in Leonor's copper-colored eyes affection resided. Her resilience amazed me.

The FARC signed a peace accord and agreed to hand in their weapons in November 2016. For Leonor, the personal was always the political. Leonor was "a reinsertada"—another government term for a former FARC trying to re-enter civilian life. Her transformations through the years were a window into Colombia's peace process: her experiences in various Colombian cities, the lowly—though legal—jobs that she was able to get, for she lacked basic education, balancing motherhood while healing from past traumas, her neighbors repudiating her once they found out she had been a FARC member. If Leonor withstood all this, and she was able to build a stable life for herself and her daughters, she was an example proving that Colombia might have a chance at peace. But, of course, each former combatant had her own path and her own monsters to overcome.

As part of the peace treaty, FARC leaders were guaranteed ten seats in Colombia's congress. The new legislators were sworn in on July 7, 2018.[4] The way Leonor told it, some of these men—the new congressmen—were atop of a pyramid of sexual tormentors. For the most part, the men in the FARC regarded girls and young women as possessions to be passed around, and the youngest and prettiest were selected for the leaders. Surely, you could not expect these men to legislate on behalf of women or children.

The Leonor I first met was petite, her body emaciated. Her manners were rehearsed to highlight slight sexual overtones: she sat cross-legged with her skirt hiked up, she tossed her head so as to flip her hair, her laugh was loud and provocative, all which made you understand—the more she revealed about her past—that older men had stolen her childhood innocence. Was her behavior the result of years of withstanding sexual and verbal abuse from Commander Tico?

Commander Tico's tyranny caused her nightmares, even a decade later. "During the day, he treated me like a queen. I was the princess. But at night, I became the worst rat. Lower than a cockroach. He raped me in all forms, anally, through the mouth. I was an object to him. I have worked very hard with psychologists to be able to see it this way. He made me bleed. He was a pervert with me. I still have nightmares that I am being raped."

How many other men had there been?

Another day, she elaborated: "My psychological damage was huge. I could have spoken to you, at first, about many things, but I always had in mind what I could not say—that I was raped numerous times, that I knew about the money, that they moved cocaine. Those were things I could not talk about."

I could not reconcile that had I been born in Leonor's hamlet and not in Bogotá, her life might have been mine.

Friends asked me: What kind of friendship can you have with a guerrillera?

As I did every few months, I dialed Leonor's telephone number, one of many she gave me through the years. If she picked up, and she was alone, she might feel free to talk. It was a cell phone, her boyfriend's, perhaps. Even after Commander Tico's abuse, Leonor always had a boyfriend, or a lover, or a fling. During the sunshine of her youth, from the way she put herself together—the girl certainly had powers to make a T-shirt allude to the fantasy of a ball gown—grown men desired her. With age and a more mature perspective dawning, she dismissed men who had passed through her life for the scavengers they were.

The dial tone confirmed the call was going through. I knew she would be limping towards the phone, the hand with the L tattoo on the wrist reaching for the receiver.

"Hola, Paula. Nunca usted se imaginará!" she said. In her voice were stalling inflections inherent of her region in Southern Colombia. There had been a death in her family, but she was equally concerned that her girls' puppy was lost. The puppy made Rosa and Dahlia happy.

Leonor's voice revealed her frenzied state—"Dios mio! Tanto ha pasado." The phone connection echoed her nervous giggles.

Since early morning she was scouting every street in Mocoa to find the puppy. Leonor was like other mothers, who found meaning and responsibility in caring for children, and who would do whatever it took to shield them; this was remarkable given all the anguish she had endured from early age. Leonor's tender disposition persisted over the time I knew her. We aged. Leonor's beauty vanished. Drained from her was the glowy youth, the cheery display. Instead, in her smile, I detected disenchantment and faded hope. We were—now—both mothers, and it was heartwarming to hear that her Rosa and Dahlia were healthy and attending school. We both were occupied with dinners to cook, laundry to wash, the tidying up. Keeping up theatrics was beyond us. We set mere minutes aside for me to telephone, stealing some time, until one of our daughters beckoned—she was hungry, and could she get some paper and crayons to draw? Or she wanted to change the channel on the TV, because there was again the story of La Llorona. Our girls' fears were the same.

According to legend, the phantom La Llorona makes ominous appearances under the moonlight by a lake or a river. Her crying conveys the pain borne by mothers.

Porqué llora?

She drowned her children and so she weeps.

Farmers speak of her when kneading bread or mending clothes.

She is a native. Tall and dark-haired.

I heard she is white.

She spooks the animals in the darkness of the night.

Words exchanged in whispers, even when there is no one who might overhear. At times of lassoing cattle in the open plains. Or when pushing past the tediousness of plucking feathers off a chicken.

She shows up to abduct our children. To replace hers, the ones she herself drowned. That is why she weeps.

No. The woman weeps for all of our lost children.

She is most often spotted in the lonesomest of places.

CHAPTER ONE

Some of the background for this chapter can be found in Arturo Alape, *Tirofijo: los sueños y las montañas* (Santafé de Bogotá: Planeta, 1994) and *Las Vidas de Pedro Antonio Marín Manuel Marulanda Vélez Tirofijo* (Santafé de Bogotá: Planeta, 1989).

Additional background found in Jacobo Arenas, Diario de la resistencia de Marquetalia (Colombia: Abejo Mono, 1972). Further details from Carlos Arango Zuluaga, *Guerrillas FARC-EP: cronicas y testimonios de guerra* (Santafé de Bogotá: Ediciones Anteo Ltd., 1984).

Leonor's parents owned a small farm, situated in a lush green hamlet—many miles from anywhere—in southern Colombia. The nearest village was Puerto Guzman. Leonor was born here in 1984. That was what her mother told her. Leonor was a toddler, and she was banging pots and pans in her parents' kitchen on the day Mercedes peered out the window and saw the FARC militias ambling in the direction of the house. There they were, a handful of teens in FARC fatigues, and Mercedes was, truthfully, not surprised. After all, this was FARC country, and everyone had a relative, or at least knew of someone, in the FARC.

The FARC teens appeared a tad older than Mercedes's eldest children, certainly not older than fifteen. From behind the window, Mercedes studied them: their conversation was punctuated with smiles. They joked, and they flirted with one another in the shy ways that young people do. Each held an AK-47, but none of the rifles pointed in a menacing way. One boy was using his as a walking stick.

What harm could they do? Mercedes assumed they would help themselves to the family's reserves of rice, or to one of the hogs Oliverio had raised since it was a piglet. This is what FARC members had done at neighboring farms.

Oliverio was working the fields, and in the distance he appeared diminutive, his brown hat blending in with his surroundings. His head down, he axed the soil, readying to plant potatoes by next week. He had talked to Mercedes about the ways he would make the land profitable. He planned to get a loan from the government and expand by buying out the neighbors. Oliverio looked up, for the first time noting the FARC's arrival. He dropped the axe and ran towards the FARC with the intention to intercept them before they reached the house. Mercedes understood that there was cause to panic.

Mercedes accounted for her children: Leonor and Leo were next to her, and nearby, the latest newborn napped inside a basket. Milton—nearing nine years old, but quick-minded and wise beyond his years—was cleaning the stable, the domain of the family's two horses. Would the FARC depart with one of the animals, or both? Where were the older girls, Adelaida, Ligia and Consuelo? What if a FARC member forced himself on one of the girls?

Milton reached the FARC before Oliverio, and he took control. He shook hands with some of the teens in fatigues. They could have just as well been his chums, playing soccer or exchanging stories about girls. There was head-nodding from both sides—look at that! Look at the boy Milton diffusing the situation—and Mercedes could breathe again. She had remained standing by the kitchen window, holding the newborn in her arms, afraid the baby might cry and startle the armed boys. Oliverio, looking haggard joined the group outside. Within minutes, the FARC departed.

They had come to warn the family—abandon your land, or else. At the time, Leonor was three years old. The way Mercedes told it, the FARC were after the family's farm because it was in a corridor between drug trafficking routes.[1] FARC top commanders, including one known as Sureshot, so called for his accuracy with a gun, controlled swaths of land by force.

Threats, displacement, property theft, poverty. Acts of war dominated Colombia's countryside for generations. As a nineteen-year-old, Sureshot himself had been displaced from his Uncle Manuel's coffee farm.[2] One evening in 1947, at dusk, Sureshot was weighing sacks of coffee beans when he heard his sister's cry.[3] Her lament—Auxilio!—was faint. Sureshot rushed to her, but freelance assassins—termed "Pajaros" (Birds)—had already gang-raped her. She lay bleeding, and Sureshot watched her take her last breath. Strapped to her chest was a note from the Birds: Stop killing Conservatives.

Sureshot and his family lived in Tolima department, a traditional haven for Liberals, and her murder was an act of retaliation for voting Liberal. The assassins had begun flying into hamlets and towns (as forsaken from government assistance as Leonor's) in 1946, shortly after a right-winger Conservative president—who conformed to US anti-Soviet policies—took office.[4] The Birds intended to wipe out the Liberal Party, which veered in the direction of trade unions and social reforms, and was colluding with the underground Communist Party. The Birds referred to the locals as "chusme," or "vermin"—and naturally Sureshot understood the term defined how the government in Bogotá viewed communities like his, as cockroaches or fleas or rats to be exterminated. It established his lifetime distrust in the State and its institutions, an idea—perhaps more than an idea, a policy—that he ingrained in successive generations of FARC members.

On the day his sister was murdered, Sureshot saw smoke surging from the family's home. The Birds had set it on fire before they galloped off with the family's cattle, mules, medicine for livestock, harnesses, and kitchenware. What was the family to do?

The next evening, by candlelight (there was no electrical infra-structure in the isolated area), Sureshot's community pro-claimed him their leader. He was the oldest of his siblings, and he took responsibility for their protection.[5] Gone were his dreams to expand the coffee plantation. It was one hundred hectares and produced thirty-five sacs of coffee per season, which was considered successful.[6] In a climate of Birds and anti-Communism politics, a Conservative government would never consent to give Liberal landowners like his family a loan.

Sureshot moved about in the bush, where he found his neighbors were in hiding. He learned his sister was not the only victim.[7] Birds were attacking pregnant women, cutting out their babies, and leaving the women for dead. Birds were frisking locals at random as they moved about their vicinity, and blocking the delivery of food to the entire region. Locals were receiving death-threat letters, illustrated with a knife or a funeral wreath drawn in blood.

Concealed in the foliage, Sureshot overheard the Birds' dialects and discerned they had been sent from other parts of Colombia, from the cities, Medellin or Bogotá. He smelled their cookout, meat and yucca. He was surviving on roots and water.

Sureshot's community came together to fight back. The men stole arms from the Birds.[8] They developed signals—clothes left tied on fences of abandoned homes communicated that the comrades were in a nearby trench.[9] The machete carving of a slanted "X" on a branch said that the comrades had moved on to the next point where they agreed to meet.[10] Family members who were not in hiding concocted gun powder from household cooking and cleaning products including salt and charcoal.[11] Mothers sent children to play in the patios of police stations, and so to eavesdrop.[12]

Indeed, Sureshot witnessed the fiercest fighting, which took place in his region in Tolima department.[13] It was in this climate that Sureshot—passing from young adult to middle-age— formed his habits and thoughts, his peculiarities and fears. What he lived during this era, later known as "La Violencia," formed his principles for FARC leadership—take action, don't let your guard down, anticipate the enemy's plans, distrust even your closest comrades, and never sleep in the same place on consecutive nights.

Leonor's parents understood Sureshot's threat. Mercedes packed. By dawn, a wagon, hitched to the two horses, was stacked with mattresses, chairs and tables. And pots, pans, and cups were tied to the sides of the wagon. The family surrendered their home.

The older children helped the parents carry the babies. The wagon wasn't sturdy. Pieces of its cargo fell off and left a trail, a baby's bottle, a shoe, a saucer, a spoon. Oliverio's mind lingered on the plans he'd envisioned for his land. Milton felt anger, his spirit already bent on revenge. There seemed no end to their walk.

In one decade—between 2006 and 2016—more than seven million Colombians were displaced from their homes, more than in Syria, Iraq, or any other war zone.[14]

"Toco dejar todo botado. Toco andar," Leonor told me.

They left everything behind, and how could their lives go on? While the sun sank, Milton helped Oliverio to lay a mattress on the ground, and Mercedes did what she could to clean up the younger ones and settle them for the night.

When Sureshot first went into hiding, he was single. He had been young, optimistic, and entrepreneurial. Sometime during the twenty years wandering the countryside, from town to town, evading the Birds, he found a steady partner and had five children. Permanent signs of exhaustion and suffering formed around his eyes. His back humped. In 1962, in his mid-thirties (he didn't have a birth certificate, and only guessed his age) he found refuge in an abandoned farm, "Marquetalia." Other refugee families he'd vowed to look after also made their way to the farm.

The families cleared land and planted sugarcane, coffee, bananas, corn, and beans.[15] They built houses—with dirt floors and thatched roofs—and each family partitioned a piece of land to raise cattle and pigs. They cooked over wood fires. Their light came from candles and kerosene lamps. Sureshot grew a mustache and filled a paunch. He wore fatigues and a cap with its visor turned up.

Colombian State intelligence reports said all civilian authorities in the Communist enclave of Marquetalia answered to Sureshot. Anyone who entered or left the region had to get a permit from him. Reports also said that Sureshot recruited teen-aged foot soldiers, and extorted "taxes" from locals, a cow here, a bucket of milk there.[16]

The US government asked, Would Colombia become another Cuba? Sureshot prepared his community for the attack he knew would come. The families dug trenches to connect the warrior communes. The men trained in marches, formations, and target shooting. The women stored extra food.

In May 1964, as the Colombian government's military surveillance airplanes closed in above the mountains of Marquetalia, Sureshot gathered the families and rushed them to one of the highest peaks. Pigs and sheep were brought up the mountains. Fog and dense plant life made the mountains an ideal hiding place. The mules carried burlap sacks filled with coffee, soap, blocks of salt, and coal for the cooking fires. Cabbage and carrots were atop boxes containing dynamite. Heavy rains turned paths into precipices and landslides, and mules went tumbling down. All dogs were slain, lest they barked.

In the valley below, government soldiers torched homes. Sureshot's community numbered one thousand men, women and children, but there were arms only for forty-eight.[17] After dusk, a flashlight beaming on the ground three times identified a comrade.[18] With the battery-powered radio at his ear, Sureshot half-dozed, attentive for updates. Via Radio Havana and Radio Moscow, Communist guerrillas aided one another across the globe.[19]

The government army's airplanes persevered with surveillance, and with each passing day, more appeared. They dropped flyers announcing a bounty on Sureshot's life. Other flyers said, "Give yourself up."

A young man said, Give up and go where? To Bogotá, to peel potatoes in some rich household? I'll stay here and fight.

Sureshot ordered the women and young children to evacuate through the bush. To the men, he said, Compañeros, the thing here is not about who is the most macho, or who is the individual hero. Here it is about organized fighting. We will sustain our fire and triumph, little by little.[20]

At dawn on June 15, 1964, government planes dropped bombs near camp. The ground shook every few minutes. In the distance, government soldiers were cutting down trees, and minutes later, sixteen thousand well-equipped elite fighters—trained in Fort Bragg, North Carolina—landed.[21] Next, two hundred and fifty of the government's most skilled fighters parachuted from DC-3 and C-47 planes. The army had helped an Indian chief with his health problems, and so earned his trust. His clan helped the army to locate and attack Sureshot's band in the mountains.

For days, Sureshot's men fired down on and blocked the government troops, and when Sureshot's men ran out of ammunition, they dispersed and regrouped in Riochiquito.[22] On his battery-powered radio, Sureshot listened to the commander of the government's Armed Forces declaring that the government again had regained control of Marquetalia.[23]

Soon, the survivors of Marquetalia and their Communist sympathizers baptized themselves the Revolutionary Armed Forces of Colombia, the FARC. They formalized their alliance with the Communist Party and proclaimed themselves its official military arm. Four decades after its inception, the FARC continued an annual celebration of the sacrifices made during the battle of Marquetalia. Leonor remembered the yearly event as a night of dancing and drinking under the stars.

After their first farm was stolen, Leonor's family wandered in the bush. Malnourished, through bouts of illness, they finally found refuge in a jungle settlement called Los Azules, on the banks of a river near the hamlet of Puerto Leguizamo.

Conditions in the settlement were primitive. Mothers and children died during childbirth. Tuberculosis was rampant. Survival meant working together with other refugee families.[24] They shared shelter, mostly under the canopy formed by lush trees. They helped each other pick wild fruits, shrubs, buds from palms, and mushrooms that were safe to eat. Together, they hunted small animals. Everyone took turns tending to a fire and stirring the communal cooking pot.

The government speculated that in such settlements, there were guerrilla sympathizers, and guerrillas in hiding. Indeed, there were FARC camps scattered here and there, and the entire area was overtaken by drug trafficking. Sureshot and the FARC Secretariat felt safe enough to build a headquarters, the Green House, which was a play on the White House and on the tree tops that concealed them from air surveillance. The Green House hosted top-level meetings with emissaries of Venezuelan dictator Hugo Chavez, international arms dealers, and drug traffickers.

CHAPTER TWO

Some of the background for this chapter can be found in Vera Grabe, *Razones de Vida* (Bogotá, D.C.: Editorial Planeta Colombiana, S.A.: February 2001).

Until the 1990s, the FARC was contained mostly in rural areas. In the 1980s in the cities, before there was talk of the FARC, the chat around terror was caused by the M-19, the Movement 19th of April, a completely different group. It was from M-19 that FARC learned to take the conflict to the cities, and into the neighborhoods where the political and business leaders were raising families. Since before I was born, during the years when my grandfather's business took off—as his company transformed the first of his pastures into houses and apartment buildings and new neighborhoods—our family was forced to hire armed bodyguards. My parents frequently met with experts from the State security agency, DAS, and since adolescence, my brother, Alejandro, was included. I was not. One day, as a kid, I watched my father close the door behind them when the security experts came. There was no way to eavesdrop. They were discussing threats posed by M-19. It was 1982.

"You want to tell me what that was about?" I asked Alejandro once, after my father opened the door again.

"Not really," he said.

He saw that I was looking at his face in alarm, my eyes wide, growing wider. "They did not say much," he said. Then he mumbled, "Or at least not much for a little girl to know. Go play with Tata." Tata was my nanny.

"What does that mean?" I asked.

He walked away, but momentarily turned back, and he nodded, in the way a man might do, troubled by thought, though his athletic clothes, his lanky body, and his shaggy haircut were a teen's. I saw he was vulnerable. It took me a minute or two to realize that something said behind closed doors had upset him.

I was startled. My face tingled and my legs felt hollow.

Behind us, at the rim of our hearing, my father was thanking the security guys for coming. He bid them goodbye with a brief half-smile that was perhaps not for them at all, but for his children.

Later, I was shocked to read that the M-19 conducted informal meetings over ice-cream at Chicos on Bogotá's Calle 85.[1] Tata and Angel, my childhood bodyguard, sometimes rewarded me with ice-cream at Chicos after my ballet lessons down the street. Had we ever shared a table at Chicos with M-19s? A trip to Chicos was a rare outing into Bogotá's public spaces.

As a child, I had few occasions to wonder without bodyguards. But inside the grounds of "El Country," as we called our club on Carrera Quince near Unicentro mall, I was free to be alone. No personal security was allowed to enter past the two kiosks where the club's guards checked membership cards, and a dog sniffed for explosives.

The Olympic-sized pool was intimidating, with flags hanging above the lanes to mark the distance. We marveled at the fourteen-foot-high trampoline, and at the water that turned a darker hue of blue the closer it was to the deep end. This is where La Llorona drowned her children, one of us commented. We nicknamed the lifeguard "Pelé," after the Afro-Brazilian soccer player. We emerged from the pool pruney, our teeth chattering, and "Pelé" wrapped towels around us. Ravenous, we snacked on Chocolatinas Jet, or ordered a portion of salchipapas, half french fries and half cut-up hot dogs, which we dunked in "salsa golf," a mix of mayonnaise and ketchup.

Most of us bowled for hours in the basement where Señor Miranda fitted us with bowling shoes before we could even tie our shoelaces. Some of us celebrated our birthdays at the club's playground, decorated with giant streamers and helium balloons. Anita, who had eyes on everything and everyone, often scolded the boys to behave. Some of us returned from the mall in Miami with Strawberry Shortcake dolls whose vinyl hair we combed obsessively. One of us had the Barbie playhouse. Most of us were studying English in the American or the British school. We knew the names of every American state but we could not recite the Colombian departments.

Some of us kept horses in the club's stable and rode after school every day, religiously. One of us competed internationally, and he travelled to Panama. His photo was printed in *El Tiempo* newspaper. Many more of us took tennis lessons but none was ever very good. A few of us played squash. One of us played golf with his father every weekend. Some of us snuck in to see our grandmothers playing Canasta in the "no kids allowed" area, and emerged with red lipstick on our cheeks.

The Bogotá I knew was an insulated world. We barricaded ourselves to stay safe from the unrest growing around us.

Around this time, Javier, who would much later become the social worker in charge of the child soldier division for the Ministry of Family Welfare, had been an M-19 member in Bogotá. By the time I met him, Javier wore wrinkled white button-down shirts, and the way his small oval spectacles slid down his nose, it was easy to picture him as a boy who loved to read. Javier often carried a sack made by Colombian natives, and in it he kept notebooks in which he scribbled his thoughts. At one time, he referred to me as "a gentle soul," seemingly as an afterthought, and in his intonation, I was baffled whether he meant it as a compliment. I respected that, though he could have secured a higher-paying job, he chose to stay with the children's ministry. His bosses were politically appointed and they came and went, but Javier was a constant, and he ran the youth demobilization program.

Once, he warned me, "What the teens tell you, you will need to peel and peel, like an onion, and at the center, is some truth." His voice flowed in squeals, though faint and muffled.

"How so?" I asked.

"You will see," he said, "or you might not."

Javier was the son of a small factory owner, and throughout his childhood his father made him work at the factory. The way Javier dropped this fact about himself into our conversation indicated how he thought of his situation: you were born into your station. He viewed me as one of the country-club elite.

I found out, sometime later, that Javier mocked me with those within his circle for not fully grasping the nuances of their guerrilla world. This information surfaced when I met with a politician, a former guerrilla himself, who informed me what Javier had told him about me: "Shallow." "Uninformed." "Biased." "A Country Club kid." Javier denigrating me had his desired effect—certainly, I was made to feel out of place in my own country.

In 2016, Javier drove a two-door Mazda. He gave me a ride once or twice, while Juaquin, the bodyguard then in charge of me, of course, followed behind in the bulletproof SUV. Javier was tall, his knees chafing against the wheel. He was a conscious driver. He maintained both hands on the wheel, and when he turned corners, his entire torso turned as well. In the car with him, the uncanniness of the moment was not lost on me; he was a former M-19, and in any foreseeable future—given the peace process signed with the FARC in 2016—would there ever be a scenario in which I would voluntarily get in a car driven by a former FARC?

In 2001, Colombian intellectuals helped me set up a meeting with Javier's former M-19 leader, Vera Grabe.[2] She was once a top commander. I organized our meeting on the pretense that I was a freelance reporter for *Maclean's* magazine. Nine years prior, the M-19 had signed a peace accord, and Vera was granted immunity from her role as one of only two women in the group's leadership.[3] From what I had read, she seemed the most rational and the most approachable of all the former M-19 leaders. But as a woman, how did she navigate rising through the ranks of a male-dominated armed group?

In the hallways leading to Vera's office, the whispers followed me: "She's blonde, she must be Vera's daughter." "She and Vera have the same blue eyes."

Vera's front teeth dented inwards and met inside her mouth to form a V. Her hair, once blonde and now white, was cut short and curls were beginning to grow in. The skin on her face was freckled from years of damage. Vera began by telling me that hatred has to do with fear, and fear comes from ignorance or arrogance. Facing her, I burnt with fear. She explained that her participation in M-19 arose from a love for people.

Two years before I was born, in 1972, Vera Grabe was twenty years old when she decided to take up arms and launch a socialist revolution. She made the decision on a damp afternoon in Bogotá when she was volunteering to teach adult literacy in a slum. The classroom was a shack with punctured brick walls and a zinc roof, and it was nearly destroying Vera to witness the fading hopes of the poor. Her students were day laborers, bricklayers, mechanics, artisans, shop keepers, and single mothers. Anger assaulted Vera when she peered in their homes, with dirt floors, communal outhouses, and electricity hijacked from city lampposts.[4] Her students bought their water from wagons pulled by mules, and their children were malnourished. To do nothing to help them would be inhuman. She felt she could not do enough.

She shared her indignation with her classmates at La Nacional University. Many, like Vera's literacy students, were from the countryside and it had been an effort for them to migrate for school. Her classmates were the Mao followers in black ponchos and black rubber boots, Che's admirers in black berets, and the Trotskyites with small frameless eyeglasses. They told Vera, Pay attention, Blondie, change is happening in the Soviet Union, China, Cuba, and North Korea. Change comes only when the social and political framework is replaced, compañera. Because the oligarchs, comrade, lack social sensibility.[5] One moment, Vera was in love with her peers; the next moment, they discriminated against Blondie—

bourgeois spy!—because she graduated from El Andino, Bogotá's German private school. Compañeros and comrades taunted her for enjoying Jorge Luis Borges and Pablo Neruda, for praying and for speaking German, which she'd learned from her immigrant parents. Soon, her classmates became a source of anguish and pressure.

It was the time of the Cold War, and because La Nacional University was known as a Communist nesting ground, there was some repression. Classes were often cancelled because students and professors were throwing rocks at the police, and the police responded with tear gas. Suspicion and hostility permeated Vera's circle: Maoists attacked all Trotskyites as traitors. Cubans yelled that Maoism was not for Latin America. The ambience of the campus contributed to Vera's low self-esteem because she could not find acceptance in any group of friends.

Yet Vera continued with her commitment to a socialist revolution. She gave in to her father and transferred to the private and much calmer Los Andes University (also my father's alma mater). Early in the semester, one afternoon in January 1974, she brought home social activists who also volunteered in the slum. She sensed her father taking in their rural accents and ratty clothes, and she read his thoughts: Los Andes students drive BMWs and wear cashmere sweaters, who were these friends of Vera? But Vera was following Che's number one rule of guerrilla warfare: compartmentalization. As few people as possible needed to know what you were doing. Vera often left the house at five in the morning and told her father she had an early class. She received random phone calls, carried out in whispers or code words, after which she took the car keys and disappeared for hours. She was the only one in the group with access to a car. Her clandestine life included graffitiing walls to protest the murder of Salvador Allende, target shooting, and discussions of the writings of Mao, Che, and Fidel. The pistol she was asked to guard, locked in a drawer in her dresser, excited her: "Power comes from the barrel of a gun."

Vera told her father she and her friends were going to work on a school project, and she rushed the group into her bedroom. She locked the door. Simon and Garfunkel blocked out their voices. She had hidden her cello because another social activist, Benjamin, had said, Blondie, you were brought up with the cello while I was lullabied with the kena. Among them, it was important to identify your social class, and Vera was at a loss: too rich for La Nacional and too poor for Los Andes. She told me that she also did not consider herself Colombian enough because of her German background; her parents immigrated to Colombia before Vera was born.

The group had been convincing her for weeks to spy on her classmates from Los Andes. To hurt the rich was the only way for things to change, one said. Only Vera had access to them, another added. But Vera had resisted because Los Andes remained the only place where she was a normal student.

Vera cleared her throat. Now, I will spy on the oligarchs in Los Andes, she said. I thought about it and I will do it.

A few high-fived each other. The group drank coffee from one mug and they passed it around, lip to lip, until it reached Vera's. Vera glowed. Their acceptance granted her a sense of belonging.

The compañeros around her bed became her compas, her tribe, and within a year, they formed part of M-19.

As a founding member of M-19, Vera instantly became a commander, though low-ranked because she was a woman. One day, she was in a rush to get to class, and the men scoffed at her. They were friends of other M-19s, middle-class lawyers, and they fantasized about becoming rebels. They'd expected a rebel commander to arrive on a speeding motorcycle, with a beret and a leather jacket. Instead, anthropology notes flooded from her bag. The lawyers knew her as Cristina. She wore a miniskirt. Her disobedient curls jutted in all directions. She handed the men a stack of M-19 newspapers and told them to distribute them outside factories. Her timidity was apparent, and the men refused. They were meant for bigger things, they told her. After much discussion, the men agreed to set off aluminum cookie tins, filled with explosives and M-19 newspapers, in movie theaters. The explosives were minuscule, enough to pop the lid and flush the papers out like a tiny volcano. When they reported back a week later, Vera found it endearing the way the men's faces lit up. They were like kids playing. A month later, she had the men running five miles per day. During Holy Week, under her supervision, the lawyers hijacked dairy delivery trucks and distributed milk to children in slums.[6] In her spare time, Vera was learning to handle the pistol.

Vera did the minimum to pass her classes at Los Andes. Meanwhile, she wrote for the M-19 newspaper, developed physical strength, and mastered target-shooting. One day in March 1978, her father held her diploma in his hands. He was a carpenter of high-end furniture. He made decent pay and he'd saved to pay her tuition, and now, the government was contracting Vera to gather data from the countryside. For her, it was the ideal cover—plus, a paycheck.

The job of the revolutionary leaders, wrote Fidel and Che, is to organize and so unfold the tyranny.[7] Vera took on the indoctrination of factory workers, cattle herders, and one professional cattle inseminator. They were about two decades older than her, and they told her about their childhoods, in the 1950s, when crimson rivers flushed down corpses.[8] The victims were the men's fathers, brothers and uncles, and their crime had been—literally, in some cases—to wear the color red in an oligarchic blue town. They had grown up immersed in political violence, and experienced the same heartbreaks as Sureshot when his sister was murdered. The men were early members of the Communist Youth Movement, the JUCO, and often, their question was: Commandante Vera, how best do we combine all forms of struggle?

Vera thought about the question, and during a meeting of M-19 higher-ups, she said the M-19 should be the armed sect of a legitimate political party. She suggested the ANAPO, the National Popular Alliance Party,[9] because the ANAPO shared M-19's belief in instruction of the masses, nationalization of natural resources, land expropriation in favor of campesino co-ops, state control of the central bank, and expulsion of the oligarchy! The compañeros ignored her. Unlike her, few had a college degree; most were drop-outs. But one man, Pablo, winked at her and repeated her suggestions, and then the men agreed. She'd been sharing weekday nights with Pablo but didn't know much about him.[10] He was nicknamed the Twig because he was scrawny. His nose was like a beak. He would tell Vera, No, I can't tell you where I'm going, so that on Friday afternoons he could freely go see his wife, Esmeralda, and their two daughters.[11] His real name was Jaime Bateman, and he was M-19's leader, famous for having defected from the FARC after his public disenchantment with FARC ideologists.[12] FARC was a radical peasant self-defense movement that believed change would come from the countryside while the M-19 was comprised of urban middle-class university students who thought bringing the conflict to the cities and stirring the political and economic establishment—via violence—would force changes. The uncle of a top M-19 commander was the government defense minister, and he referred to the M-19 as "kids acting out."

The revolution is a party! said the Twig one evening. Everyone drank Cuba Libres.[13] You have to be crazy, the Twig said, passionately crazy!

Another man said, Viva the Eme! The muchachas of the Eme are the best-looking girls!

Women were told to wear miniskirts to distract the enemy. Vera's uniform included oversized jeans. In the M-19, no one wore fatigues.

One guy pinched Vera's behind; another would punish her because she rejected him.

M-19's rank and file soon discovered Vera's relationship with Jaime, and the whispers began, She's ranked only because she's one of the Twig's girls. It was standard that M-19 members swapped lovers every few months. When loneliness gripped Vera because the Twig was with his wife, she consoled herself, Why would I want to be stuck in stereotypical roles that society assigns to women? Still, she longed for a child, and soon, radiant as a full moon, she announced she carried the Twig's baby. But the M-19's male leadership—including the Twig—reprimanded her. It was time, they said, to liberate women from domestic slavery![14] La Comandante must think of herself as a statesperson. She felt hatred and envy, too, because the Twig and other men in the Eme were free to be commanders and fathers while their wives and girlfriends raised their children. The rage built inside her. Yet, Vera, four months pregnant, did what the Twig ordered and aborted her child. She regretted it her whole life, holding on to fantasies of how it might have been to raise their baby. For eight years until his death in a plane accident, she struggled to keep up a relationship with the Twig.[15] Despite it all, or perhaps because of his early death, she called him the love of her life.

Vera told me she was like a mother or a wife who gives herself up for her family. The Eme's were her family. While others followed compartmentalization and hid behind masks, hats and sunglasses, Vera went about freely and took on more risk. She hid M-19 newspapers and plans of government buildings in her apartment. She falsified ID cards. She volunteered her car, for whatever mission.

Commander Vera Grabe was arrested at five-thirty p.m. on October 26, 1979—during rain season; the newspapers printed news of her detention alongside photos of zinc-roofed huts swallowed by landslides. Weeks prior, the compas had stolen nearly six thousand arms from a military arsenal.

The interrogator asked, Where are the stolen arms? She wouldn't talk.

The compas were smuggling them to the Sandinistas in Nicaragua. Marx wrote: Proletariats of all countries, unite![16]

Vera was barefoot and the floor of the improvised cell in a horse stable in Bogotá's Thirteenth Military Brigade was wet and cold. The mildewed blindfold squeezed her eyeballs. She felt herself being lifted—the handcuffs clicked, and she hung from a rod. The blanket dropped and she was left naked.

The interrogator asked, Why are there stamps for Panama in your passport? The authorities had searched her apartment.

The more blows she received, the less she felt her body.

The others talked, the interrogator said.

Breaking down would be worse than death.

Next, her head was covered with a pillowcase and dunked for a few seconds in the horses' drinking fountain. Sometimes the interrogators showed up without masks; did that mean they would kill her?

The night guard was of high school age. Occasionally, furtively, jittery, he brought her a cup of hot chocolate and a piece of cake, Vera's only food in days. Please, eat quickly, señora, he said.

The cries of the compa, of a male commander, in the stable next to hers were like a stab, and Vera began to sing: boleros, childhood songs, nursery rhymes, whatever crossed her mind. Nine years later, the man thanked her.

On Halloween night, two men with alcohol breath and a boombox came into her cell and cackled something about a witch hunt. They blindfolded her again, and tore the blanket away from her. Rock music blasted. They pinched her breasts and kicked her in the stomach. She told me that she repeated to herself, My body is one thing, my mind is another. They next flung her on the floor and shoved a broomstick up her vagina. She was sweating and panting. She heard them talking about raping her. Breathe, she told herself, waiting for something or someone to change the horror, make it all right again. Vera told me she'd seen one of the rapists not long before we talked and she felt nothing, but when she said it her face flushed.

The incident with the broomstick caused her to bleed for some time; ten days later, when Commander Vera Grabe was tried and found guilty of rebellion and sentenced to one year in "the Good Shepherd," Bogotá's women's prison, she still could not sit upright. Vera had not broken down though a few compas blamed their imprisonment on her. Even so, she felt much community with the rest of the political prisoners. Her father visited every Sunday and brought her meat and potato balls, which he'd spent all day on Saturday cooking. Vera was relieved to tell him everything—he said, Hija, is it true what they tell me? My daughter is a *commander*! That is more than I've done with my life. Her father's approval got her thinking, and prison gave her months to think. Reading the Bible, knitting, cooking, washing her clothes, walking the patio back and forth—plenty of time to decide what was to come. After six in the afternoon, the cells were locked, and Vera, stretched out on a mattress under a white lightbulb, thought: We will move forward on the path of the revolution, on the path of socialism, on the path of Marxism-Leninism. Nation or Death! We will win! Her father demanded that if she were to remain in the M-19, she had to leave the country for a few years after her release. She agreed with him. He died before the two saw each other again.

Weeks after her release from prison, she became M-19's international liaison because she was the only one with a German passport. The waves of the Pacific crashed into the wooden fishing boat. Three days passed: green reefs on the right, the horizon on the left, and the fisherman dropped Vera off in Panama. Proletariats of all countries: unite! She traveled to Cuba, Nicaragua, Panama, Mexico, Chile, Ecuador, Costa Rica, Peru, Venezuela, Germany, France, Spain, and Italy, and Vera did what she could—Fidel on her mind: Unite because of the class enemies, the imperialist enemies!—as long as the male contacts did not ask her to continue the meeting in a motel room. Away from the compas, during the brief visits to her mother in Hamburg, Vera picked up the cello again. With the bow vibrating the strings, the cellist returned to childhood, to the afternoons in Bogotá when a scrawny curly-blond girl towed a cello uphill and mounted the streetcar to her weekly lesson at the National Conservatory.

In 1984, Vera returned to Colombia. As a commander, she was required to spend time in the mountains with the masses, biding the moment to march triumphantly into the cities. Patria o muerte![17] Venceremos! During a long march, a love note passed hand-to-hand. It was from Juan, another commander, and it was addressed to "Blondie." By the end of the week, Vera and Juan shared a tent.

The compas perceived that Vera was pregnant before she did. Juan worried. Was his baby still moving? Was Vera getting enough to eat? She continued the long hikes. In the late afternoons, after helping the compas set up camp for another night, Vera drank hot chocolate and ate rice and meat that the compas prepared. Then, she laid back to enjoy the baby leaping inside her. In the evenings, under the stars, by the fire, she cuddled with Juan. The compas serenaded and told jokes.

One morning, the army surprised them. There was heavy shooting. Vera was forced to run across a clear pasture, her heart skipping beats, both hands supporting her belly. Bullets zoomed past her and she remembered: if you can hear the bullet, it is not meant for you. That evening, she held wounded compas, calming them, waiting for them to take their last breath, all while the baby kicked inside her.

The group had to vacate the region as soon as they could. The marches now lasted sixteen hours per day or more, up mountains and down precipices. Vera held on to branches and tree roots, careful not to slip, her arms guarding her growing belly. There was not enough food, and entire days passed in which Vera starved.

Three months before Juanita's due date, on April 26, 1986, Vera's water broke. A doctor, an Eme sympathizer, risked his freedom to hide Vera in a private clinic in Medellín. Her fever surged and the contractions continued, and the sound of army choppers outside, going after the compas, churned Vera's anguish. There was no one to hold her hand. Juan was with the compas, robbing the bank vault of a nearby town, burning judicial archives, shooting down security guards and police. Then, the black memory of the torture and rape came over her. Tears blurred the clock on the wall. Juanita was premature and easy to push out. The baby was taken to a hospital incubator to be cared for by strangers, and the mother, heavy with thoughts of the other baby she'd almost had with the Twig, rushed back to her guerrilla work. Juanita was raised by her father's relatives, and she grew up to despise Vera and refused to acknowledge her. Perhaps it was because of Vera's physical absence, or perhaps because Juanita had to endure the media stories of Vera, the guerrillera, and Vera, the murderer. Once Vera told me, "I never speak about my daughter. That's my weakness."

When her assistant, Nelly, commented that I physically resembled Juanita—blue eyes, fair skin—I perceived Vera's pain, in the manner in which her head and shoulders quivered.

I felt sorry for Vera. I understood the anger that arose in her from witnessing poverty up close; when I saw sheds with punctured walls and zinc roofs, I had the same reaction—not only anger, but also grief, and, I, too, had felt that to do nothing would be inhuman. It caused me much anguish to hear Leonor's stories of fading hope.

But it was difficult for me to summon any congeniality with Vera. Her decisions as a commander had dictated the direction of my life, and she and the M-19s displaced me from my homeland.

CHAPTER THREE

For weeks in 2001, Vera and I met occasionally. She invited me to her apartment on a top floor of a high-rise in downtown Bogotá, not far from La Candelaria neighborhood. It was not cheap real estate. The living room was spacious with a lone armchair and a sofa over which she draped a cloth such as you pick up at street fairs. The remains of candles coated a side table. We sat there, opposite floor-to-ceiling windows that overlooked the bullfighting ring below. She brewed us black coffee in a French press.

Other days, we met in her office. She and another former M-19 had formed a think tank and they wrote papers and books about Colombia's challenges. They said they were experts on the subject because they'd experienced it in the frontlines. But it seemed more of a way to have a paying job as consultants and opinion-makers, and to feel less alone in the world.

"Nice to see you, Vera. Even though I can't believe I'm voluntarily spending time with you," I said one morning in the hallway to her office, and laughed. "I told you I'm a Canadian reporter. I am also Colombian."

She was puzzled, and I told her who my grandfather was. In 1970, my grandfather, Fernando Mazuera, the four-time mayor of Bogotá who commissioned projects to bring roads, transportation and running water to the slums in southern Bogotá, turned down an offer from a populist political party, the ANAPO, to run for vice-president. Three years later, in 1973, the M-19 declared themselves the military arm of the ANAPO, though the ANAPO never formally embraced them. By 1983, my grandfather's renown attracted the M-19's interest.

One evening in February 1983, the news reported the kidnapping of the daughter of one of our family's business competitors. She had been snatched from her classroom at a local university. Weeks prior, DAS, the state security agency, had warned my parents that the M-19's spies were trailing our family and studying our routines. They were aware of the times of the day when we drove to school and to the Country Club, and the routes we took. Their intention was to kidnap one of us; maybe even me, and I was then eight years old.

When my father arrived home early, he did not change into his pajamas, but instead lit a Marlboro. He spoke to my mother in English (a language I could not yet understand). His voice was deep. He dialed the rotary phone at his bedside table, a separate landline strictly reserved for his use. My mother muted the news on the television, and ordered me out of the room. My heart sank. Ice filled my stomach.

At bedtime, Mami told me we were moving to Canada. My brother was already in boarding school in Toronto, and Mami said it was a chance to see Alejandro more often. She grazed my hair with her slender, manicured fingers, the way a person feels for comfort and security. I jumped and searched the bookshelf for an atlas. My finger trailed south through north, and settled in cottage country somewhere near the Great Lakes.

For the next three days, I was confined inside the house. I took in my mother collecting mementos she could fit in a suitcase, her bedside clock, some silver frames with black and white photos of her side of the family, and an antique flower vase that once belonged to her father, the mayor.

In Toronto, my mother raised me, the school day setting the pace for our new lives. My father commuted from Bogotá every few weeks to see us. In this manner, the seasons passed. I began identifying myself as a Canadian. Dressed in a green kilt and green tights, I biked to and from school, carrying my own key and letting myself in and out of the house as I wished. Other immigrant families—from the Caribbean, India, Hungary, and Poland—became my friends.

With this in mind, I told Vera, "Your group wanted to kidnap someone in my family." I'd done it. I'd come clean. But I wasn't feeling the peace of mind I'd hoped.

Vera stayed quiet for a moment, and said, "We still fight for the same beliefs. Many things still have to change." Though she was tall and towered over me, she was gaunt and pale and had the feeble movements of old age. Her hair roots were white, her lips chapped. Blue veins popped under her eyes. She appeared vulnerable, fidgeting and pulling the ends of her sleeves to cover her hands. Her behavior said she was insecure, ready to have to defend her life choices.

"I agree we need changes," I said. In light of Leonor's life, no one could disagree that Colombia needed deep reforms. While still a minor, Leonor had faced displacement, domestic abuse, homelessness, and sexual slavery.

When Vera spoke to me about Colombians with old money and connections, she called them "arribistas," or condescending, closed-minded, highbrowed. Yet, there was some ambition in Vera to be part of that club. (In 2002, Vera ran for vice-president under the Democratic Pole, the ANAPO's heir; two generations prior, that was the political ticket my grandfather had declined, and the irony was not lost on me.) One day, when she walked me to the door, she made a joke, "I see, those are your bodyguards and not mine." She was saying, I, too, am somebody. I have bodyguards.

As I left Vera's building one afternoon, her guard, Anaide, whispered a covert invitation to coffee. Of indigenous descent and built like the karate kid, she was muscular, flat-chested, androgynous. For twenty years, since she was fourteen, she'd been in armed groups: Quintín Lame, M-19, EPL, ELN, and FARC. Now she was paid by DAS. Anaide told me that Vera made her feel insignificant. Anaide called Vera a sham. Of the groups Anaide had belonged to, the M-19 included the most middle-class urban leaders, and there was class tension between M-19 and the rural guerrilla groups. It'd been difficult for Anaide, a rural guerrilla, to receive orders from a university graduate from the city.

History revealed that the government minister's suggestion that M-19 were "kids acting out" was not accurate. It became clear that M-19 had allied with drug traffickers, including Pablo Escobar, when they took control of the Palace of Justice on November 6, 1985. In exchange for sizable payments, M-19 intended to burn judicial archives related to drug thugs facing extradition to the US.

Part of my fourth-grade homework in Toronto was to read the newspaper and follow the international news. On the evening news, I saw footage of army tanks rolling through Plaza Bolivar, Bogotá's main square. The CBC reporter explained that M-19 had taken magistrates and civil servants as hostages.

With trembling hands, my mother called my father in Bogotá. He reassured her that he had been far away from the scene.

I told Alejandro about my meetings with Vera. Vera and I were now acquaintances, though not friends, I said. Alejandro shrugged. In his work leading our family's construction business, he came across many former M-19s who went on to work in the city government.

However, if my parents had known that I met with Vera, that I heard her out, they would have thought I was a lunatic. They would have also reminded me of the details of our family friend Amalia's kidnapping.[1] *Another* kidnapping. Amalia was held for fourteen months in what the M-19 called a "prison of the people." Her crime was to be her father's daughter: He was a banker. Though the M-19 said Amalia was a political prisoner, they asked for a ten-million-dollar ransom. There was a negotiation in Panama, and a much lower number was agreed.

On July 31, 1987, Amalia, just released by her kidnappers, came to our house straight from the TV studio where Commander Vera had ordered her dropped off in the middle of the seven o'clock news. Vera chose that drop off because she feared the authorities would fire shots if Amalia was randomly released in a city intersection. As Amalia left the TV studio, cameras were thrust in her face, and so her brother-in-law drove her to our house.

Amalia's mother arrived with a hairdresser. She asked him to make her daughter blonder, to tweeze her eyebrows, to do her make-up. Amalia stood in front of a full-length mirror. Red fleabites made her thighs resemble a colander. Amalia tucked and released her gut. With disgust she recalled that she'd eaten, almost robotically, pyramids of boxes of Corn Flakes.

"Please, give me back my Amalia," her mother was telling the hairdresser. Amalia's mother was shocked that her daughter smoked and cursed.

Pop! The champagne bottles opened. Amalia's relatives and friends showed up. The Kleenex boxes passed hand-to-hand. Amalia rotated a ring on her finger. Her jewelry, zip-locked in a plastic baggy, was returned to the family at the beginning of the captivity, as part of a proof of life, and no one recognized this new ring.

Top army commanders introduced themselves to Amalia, and President Betancur called and told her she was a brave girl. The gathering was suddenly very loud and chaotic, and the flashes of the photographer for *Cromos* magazine were constant. A snap of my father's fingers ordered me upstairs, out of the photographer's reach. I was thirteen, on summer vacation from Canada.

It was Tata's scream ringing loud from the kitchen that had alerted the whole household of Amalia's arrival that day. I first heard of the M-19 one evening when I found Tata in her room, with her spectacles on, on her knees, and her elbows pinning the newspaper spread open on her bed. She was reading about the M-19. She sounded out each word. I was in first grade, about seven years old. My reading was more fluent than hers, and I was done with the article before she was. What were Tata's real thoughts and feelings about the M-19?

Tata was intelligent and a hard worker. She kept the working order of our home: she passed on the grocery list, approved by my mother, for the driver to do the bulk of the shopping; she stored the fancy plates and glasses in the storage room; and she returned the laundered sheets and towels to their rightful order inside the boxes in the linen closet. She wore a uniform, a red, fuchsia or purple housedress. On special occasions, when she served the table at a dinner party or Christmas, she donned a white apron, so starched and ironed that the fabric made tearing sounds. She kept her black hair short, all business. Beneath her stockinged legs, varicose veins protruded.

She lived with us for over thirty years. She worked six days of the week, and on her day off, she stood in lines to pay utility bills for her own house, where her daughter, her granddaughter (she was Paula, my namesake), and her sister lived. She thought of our household as her home. Her retirement was complicated: Tata wanted to stay with us, but Mami persuaded her to return to her home and reacquaint herself with her family. Her salary continued out of the love and loyalty she had generously given us through the years. During the first months that she returned to her family, she called my mother and spoke like a homesick child. I was angry at my mother; I wanted Tata to come home, but my mother was adamant that Tata must get the chance to share her final years with her family, and die amidst them.

Tata saw me reading Vera Grabe's memoir. I told her about going to see Vera.

"From the M-19?" Tata asked.

"Yes."

"In her youth, that woman lost her radar," Tata said.

It was eleven in the morning another day I came to Vera's office. She and Nelly, her assistant,[2] were eating cream cheese on rolls. Nelly was proud she'd been an M-19. But Vera berated her as just another sympathizer housewife who hid a bunch of rifles once or twice.

I pulled up a chair.

There was supposed to be an aura of terror and roaring about tall, long-limbed Vera Grabe. But I saw that all the fight was drained from her. The air around her smelled like her face cream, like roses.

"Are you glad to be home?" Vera asked. If a cat spoke, it would have Vera's voice.

"Is Bogotá home? I'm not sure anymore," I said.

"Paula, so, like how many languages do you speak?" Nelly asked.

I told them I spoke four languages. "And I have to thank Vera for that," I said. I told them that the first time I rode a bike around our new Toronto neighborhood, my mother oversaw from the window, and she felt blessed that Canada gifted her children this kind of freedom. "No bodyguards!" I said. "Gracias, Vera. I gained so much from growing up abroad."

Vera peered at me. Nelly tensed up, bringing her hand up to her mouth.

"Really, Vera. You guys opened up a lot of opportunities for me," I said, and stared into her eyes. My throat was dry.

Vera's laugh was measured. This time I was satisfied with the reaction my honesty produced in Vera.

"That settled, I have to ask you something," I said.

During our family's first months living in Toronto, my mother had hired a young Colombian woman to babysit me, to take me to the park and to the movies. Then, one day, the babysitter's mother showed up at our door early in the morning. She was in shock. She told my mother that her daughter had revealed to her, the night before, that she was an M-19 member. She did not think it was a good idea for her M-19 daughter to take care of me. I asked Vera if she remembered any M-19 members in Toronto.

"No," Vera said. "She was probably a sympathizer. After people found out that we hijacked dairy delivery trucks and distributed the milk to hungry children, we had a lot of sympathizers who called themselves M-19."

"One more question," I said.

Vera nodded.

"That kidnapping you did, Amalia. That was my friend."

Vera took her time responding. Yes, she remembered. Amalia was the hostage who assigned cardboard boxes to be pieces of furniture in the room. When Amalia told the compas she liked tea, they bought her some with their own money, and in turn, she shared it with them. And when Amalia found out she was being held by the M-19, she suggested they should raise money through bingos, raffles, and carnivals, instead of kidnappings.

"I never met Amalia," Vera said. Then she told me about one of Amalia's guards, whose nom de guerre was Camilo. He wanted to show Amalia his face without the mask, and Amalia refused. She wouldn't be forced to pick him out in a line-up later. The ring was his parting gift to Amalia.

When I left, I accepted Vera's hug. I was the only civilian who'd ever reached out to her. On the street, people shouted at her, "Guerrillera!" "Murderer!" She feared being assassinated.

I was disappointed that she had not shown remorse for kidnappings carried out by M-19. I was naive to have expected her to. She excused and justified her actions as having been inspired by a time and place in history; in much the same way, Leonor's life arose from the fact that her birthplace held the densest coca fields in the world. Victim or perpetrator. It depended whom you asked. But one thing was for certain. Minors—like Leonor—deserved to remain children as long as possible.

CHAPTER FOUR

Though the first years in Los Azules were difficult for her parents, Leonor and the rest of the children passed days playing make-belief games, climbing trees, and building huts from tree limbs. They chased butterflies and frogs, and inspected giant turtles. They graced their finger over the snouts of wild tiger cubs, hogs, and monkeys. The trickle of rainfall pattered against the foliage.

It was 1990, and Leonor was six, Leo was seven. Mercedes and Oliverio left to visit an uncle in La Hormiga, a hamlet several days distant by foot and canoe. Their weeks-long absence made Leonor and Leo fear they were abandoned—but ten-year-old Consuelo reassured them. I'll take care of you, she said.

Consuelo called them *my* children. She fed them scraps of leftovers from neighbors. She watched over them while they swam in the river and floated on inner tubes. She bathed them. In the evenings, she reenacted for them bits of scenes that she picked up from the adults' chatter.

The nights were cold and lonely in the jungle. The black hours were filled with wild animal roars, yelps, and screeches, and sometimes the hum of government military planes. Thunder clapped across the sky, and during high tide, the down-rush of the river ravaged wildlife and swallowed whole trees. In the darkness and the early morning haze, outlines were difficult to make out. There was a silhouette by the tree. Was it La Llorona?

Leonor believed she and her siblings would be drowned, or murdered. She clung to Consuelo.

I'm here, I am not going anywhere, Consuelo said.

After Oliverio and Mercedes returned from La Hormiga, their eldest son and daughter, ages fourteen and fifteen, disappeared. The FARC lured them away with promises of a salary. The teens went, knowing that the family needed money.

Mercedes pulled herself together to care for the remaining children, but what was the point?

Neighbors laid out an altar for the lost children, with flowers and statues of Jesus Christ.

Leonor had no memory of her lost brother and sister.

Oliverio had savings, and with a loan from his brother, he bought a small plot of land not far from Los Azules. He and Milton set to work, laying the foundations for a house, sowing crops, building chicken and pig coops, and budgeting for supplies for a barn for storage.

Oliverio ploughed and sowed fields.[1] Since adolescence, he'd risen before dawn, and worked all day. But increasingly now he drank. Mercedes made ends meet by cleaning and by washing other people's clothes.[2] She worked herself to exhaustion.

Mercedes realized it was no use fighting to stay afloat if she continued to get pregnant and give birth to a baby ever year. Leonor was bright-eyed. She often found empty bleach bottles, and her mother on her knees at the parish, pleading forgiveness, Escusame, Señor, escusame, Todopoderoso. In the vicinity there was nowhere to go for birth control, and Mercedes often aborted quietly on her own by squirting bleach up her vagina.[3] In the days that followed, bleeding confirmed the baby was passing. Her mother sat in the front pew every Sunday when the local Catholic priest preached that a large family was a holy family.

Leonor told me, "They always did *that*. You know what I'm saying. In front of all the children."

Mercedes's belly now showed off Baby Blanca Flor. She'd been unable to bear self-aborting this time. Her eyes crystallized with tears and then locked with Leonor's. When Mercedes was a girl, she had seen that look of doom in her own mother's gaze. The three of them, grandmother, mother and daughter, had the same eyes, like wide almonds.

I don't even want the children we have now, Leonor's father cried out. He sprang from a wooden chair, one of a few pieces of furniture besides a floppy table, rusty beds, and an ancient gas stove in the corner. The family lived in one large dusty room, always either too drafty or too stuffy.

You're a drunkard, Oliverio, Mercedes yelled. You can't hold a job.

And you're my ugly puta, Oliverio cackled, exposing his nearly bare, white gum lines. You're my angry puta, he taunted, the alcohol making him slur.

Mamá, don't cry, Leo whispered for only Leonor to hear. The two were crouched in a corner, the warmth of Leo's breath caressing his younger sister's neck. She squeezed his hand, and his tear broke onto her thumb.

Oliverio pulled his belt from his pants. Papá, don't, Leo cried, and then his cheek stung from a lash of the belt.[4]

Mercedes was standing by the opening in the wall that served as a window, and she leaped out. Theirs was one of a few buildings that had a second floor.

Milton bolted down the stairs to his mother lying in the street. She had survived, and she had no broken bones and no visible bruises.

Your mother is an ugly whore, and that's all she'll ever be, Oliverio said. He stumbled on a pot that was there to catch the rain, and after kicking it, he slammed the door behind him on his way out.[5]

Leonor and I were at a park in Bogotá where we could have privacy. The only person who came near us was a man walking a bichon frisé on a leash. I had to ask Leonor something method-ical, forcing myself to concentrate on not letting my emotion show. "Leonor, can you go through each of your siblings and tell me their ages the last time you saw them?" I asked.

"That's a hard one," she said. In light of what her home had been, she felt sorry for herself, but spoke lightly.

"You can't remember how old your siblings were?" I asked.

"I can't even remember all their names," she said. "See, I think Baby Blanca Flor came after Milady. I can't remember who came first." Milady had died when she was two months old.

"Then there was Jon Anderson. He did die in the womb. Do you want me to go through each one, even if they died already?"

I nodded.

"That's really hard, I can't remember them all." Her eyes were blank, and she wanted to turn the story to humor.

A day later, Leonor was clearer, "My mother did not want us and so what? I don't care about that."

She wanted me to know she didn't want pity.

Fifteen years later, I reminded Leonor of her mother's self-induced abortions.

Leonor said, "Dios mio, I don't know what I told you. Estaba fuera de base. I was crazy. I said *that*?—that my mother squirted bleach up her vagina?—*that* I do not remember."

She giggled.

I could not deny that the details were clear in my notes from when we first met in 2001. The way she had told it, with emotional fluctuations, was convincing, or so I had perceived; further, nearly half of a steno pad of my notes was filled with the daughter denigrating the mother.

I had heard: "I never want to see my mother again." "I don't want the government to call my mother." "I want my mother to think I am dead." Leonor had been away from her mother for five or six years—in the FARC. There had been minimal communication between them. In 2008, after seven years in government rehab, Leonor finally conceded to reconnect with Mercedes. A priority in government therapy was to reunite the families.

Leonor began forgiving her mother—and I would understand why soon enough, why Leonor felt Mercedes needed forgiving.

I asked Leonor if, perhaps, without being fully aware, she had made up an image of her mother to hide her from the FARC and so protect her. I figured the more emotional distance Leonor created from Mercedes, the less likely she talked about her when in the FARC, and the safer Mercedes was. Mercedes was, after all, her mom.

Leonor said, "No. More than protecting her, I was protecting my own freedom. I spoke to you and to the therapists very harsh things about my mother because I wanted the force of the law to fall on my mother and not me." Her voice was calm and centered.

Leonor, by then a mother herself, accepted that Mercedes was a woman dedicated to her children. Mercedes drew her deepest satisfactions from the routines of motherhood, bathing children, washing and mending clothes, deep-cleaning the house, seeing the gleam in scrubbed pots. She seemed her happiest when hearing that her granddaughters, Rosa and Dahlia, had taken their first steps, spoken their first words. It pained Leonor to know she had not recognized this side of her mother for so long.

That was not the clarity—or maturity—I had expected from Leonor. There was such growth as a result of her time spent with government psychologists. Therapy extended to family members who were willing to engage, and Mercedes helped Leonor to fill in blanks.[6]

CHAPTER FIVE

On the new farm in the hamlet of Los Azules, Mercedes did what she could to make the children feel safe and to provide a home for them.

Two years passed. It was an evening in 1992.

The family finished a dinner of rice and beans. Leo said he was still hungry.[1]

Such comments normally made Mercedes scream. This time, Milton noted the frustration and guilt in his mother's face. She was growing thinner and quieter, the life draining from her.

I can do what they've asked, Milton said. He explained he'd been approached to work picking coca leaves, and stuffing them in sacks to take to the drug labs.[2] The region that comprised Puerto Leguizamo and Los Azules and its surroundings then held the densest coca fields in the world. Milton had turned fifteen the month before, and he imagined the lavish lifestyle the cocaine industry could bring them. A single-engine plane flew in nearby once a month to drop off chemicals for the cocaine labs. The pilot stayed for an hour and took back with him cocaine worth at least five million dollars. Milton remarked on the pilot's sunglasses, and how he distributed chocolate bars to the boys. Leo had brought one back for Leonor.

With what I earn, I could help pay for stuff. My friend Jhon does it, Milton added.

Since when does Jhon do that?

Since he's no longer hungry, Mamá.

In slipping on a T-shirt, Milton was exposing his treasure-trail, no longer that of a boy's. Leonor was starting to regard him as she would an adult. One night, she'd heard Milton pleading with Oliverio. Papá, I cannot keep going out to look for you when you booze. Papá, Mamá cries when you don't come home.

Milton took on more responsibilities. He started picking coca, and the children felt safe seeing their mother's smile when he gave her the money.

One afternoon, four teenagers in FARC uniforms and carrying rifles ambled toward the house.

The leader began to speak, Vengo aquí por una razón. He slouched, as if unsure of himself. The other boys gazed intensely at him. In a week they would come back, the leader said, and el niño ought to be willing and ready.

They had come for Leo, who was within months of turning nine, a malleable age to transform him from kid to warrior. Neighbors often remarked on Leo's athleticism and agility. And he is *a good kid,* they said. Hours earlier, Leo had run barefoot to help a drug pilot to remove the leaves and tree limbs that camouflaged the plane's runway. The pilot tipped the boys for this.

Again, Mercedes took charge. She made up her mind that the FARC would not abduct Leo. This would be their second time leaving everything behind. They would move to Mocoa, the nearest large town. But Oliverio foresaw worse times to come. His body wilting, his well-worn hat in his freckled hand, he fixed his eyes on the ground. No, he would not go, his savings were gone. His brother in La Hormiga was unlikely to lend him more money. Oliverio didn't have it in him to start anew somewhere else.

"Papá abandoned Mamá to raise all the children on her own," Leonor told me. "We were all Mamá had. We had many conflicts with her. Se desquiciaba con nosotros. She was deranged. But we were her children."

Mercedes knew that after the FARC came for Leo, they would come for the others, one by one.

The family, without Oliverio, arrived in Mocoa around 1994. Leonor was ten years old, and she had not then understood that the move was to save the children from recruitment by the FARC. She remembered their dire living conditions, and she'd assumed the family moved looking for employment.

Mocoa, the capital of Putumayo department, was then an early settlement, and the family lived as squatters on an empty field at the town's periphery. They scavenged lots for discarded bricks, wooden boards, scraps of window panes, and nails, and they built temporary housing.

Mercedes took any odd job that she was offered. Setting up on a rock by the river, she hand-washed people's clothes. She left Leonor, Leo and the younger children alone, a little foot tied to the foot of the bed, like chicks in a coop, and she went to work caring for other people's children.

With her pay, Mercedes eventually built a more permanent house. First came the walls, then the roof, followed by pieces of the kitchen, the stove, and the sink. Mule-drawn carriages drove by once a week, selling water. There was an outhouse, and Leonor feared the neighbors watching her as she did her business. Years later came the indoor bathroom, and lastly, running water to replace the buckets.

At a similar pace, Mocoa expanded from large village to town to city. There wasn't a thought to urban planning, the street names and the house numbers coming after, as more squatters arrived. Most came fleeing violence.[3]

When Leonor first demobilized from FARC, she denied FARC's role in impoverishing and brutalizing people. She regarded the FARC as an extension of herself. Nor did Sureshot and other FARC admit their role in displacing countless families. Even after victims sat with FARC leaders, eye-to-eye at the peace table in Havana, and explained the atrocities FARC perpetrated, the leaders maintained that FARC was the People's Army of campesino farmers, acting in self-defense against a murderous elite. As the decades advanced, FARC's definition of murderous elite broadened to include all city people, in the same ways that M-19 had conspired. In recent years, FARC sought to attack the wealthier areas of the city in northern Bogotá. They threw explosives into a beer hall, located near popular shops and pedestrian walkways. They blew up a club where businessmen convened for lunch. My family's homes and offices were located in this area. Our routines—the market, the restaurants we frequented, and our friends' homes—naturally confined us to northern Bogotá, and we hardly had reason to wander beyond.

CHAPTER SIX

One afternoon during the first month of my meetings with Leonor, my brother and I sat in his office, an impressively spacious loft filled with artwork by young Colombians he supported. He asked me if I liked the most recently acquired piece—a series of three photographs of a half-naked woman, breasts bouncing—the photographer herself, apparently, running into the frame in the first shot and out of sight in the last. I didn't like its rawness.

"Sure, it's OK," I said, and I told him I was meeting with former child soldiers and listening to their stories. "Just be careful," Alejandro said. "We are so naive sometimes, and we should not think everyone is as naive as we are."

The breeze blew stacks of paper and several rolls of architectural plans. He had grown into his role as a businessmen profiled in magazines. Other businessmen called and asked his advice. He was a philanthropist for Bogotá's philharmonic. In his spare time, he planted and nurtured trees of various species in big pots in his terrace, and then donated them to Bogotá's botanical garden. Books were stacked on a side table in the corner, which reminded me of growing up, when he had given me books to read, not only *Lord of the Flies*, but also *To Kill a Mockingbird*, and some Hemingway.

I kneeled to pick up the fallen papers. On my knees, I was communicating that my project was, *really*, no big deal.

"I might write an article about Leonor," I said.

Alejandro paced back and forth. For the first time, I noticed his shoulders hunching. There was still a wedge between us, a residual anger and sorrow that arose in both of us after his kidnapping.

Then he signaled his agreement by smiling. I wanted to hug him, but I didn't. We kept a distance.

I was grateful for his understanding. He had returned to live in Colombia. I had not.

In the fall of 1988, my mother locked up the house in Toronto, and moved back to Bogotá. I was fourteen, old enough for boarding school.

"You're a replica of your brother," a teacher remarked.

"A male and female version of the same," a rowing coach said. It was true that our complexions were identical, as was the texture of our hair.

Alejandro and I finished growing up in dorms, which became more familiar to me than my parents' home. The families of my Canadian friends took me in for Thanksgiving and Easter. Every Sunday at nine o'clock, my grandmother, Helena, called me on the dorm's payphone. I would picture her in La Sabana in her salon, overlooking the garden, a whiskey in hand, cubes of ice building condensation around the glass.

By then, Alejandro was in college in Philadelphia. I visited him on school breaks. We spoke on the telephone every other day. One morning, I picked up my mail at the school P.O., and there was a package from him with a sweatshirt, "Wharton" printed across the chest. Next came a package from him with a Bavarian fedora. Alejandro and I maintained our bond despite hardly ever being together. When we returned to Colombia to see our parents during the holidays, we kept each other company. We read, side by side, each our own book, late into the night. We agreed that *Catcher in the Rye* captured the ambience of our dorms in Canada.

"Like when a helluva sonuvabitch comes in your room and he picks up your stuff, picture frames or what not," he said, "and comments about the photo, although the sonuvabitch has seen it a thousand times. Goddam. Get out of my room."

"Ha! Which always kills me, if you want to know the truth. It's so phony," I said.

"So phony," he repeated.

Those days in dorm rooms, when I thought of *my* family, it was time spent in "Santa Nena"—during the three months of summer—that I longed for. Santa Nena was my parents' country house. Though early mornings and evenings were cold, by noon, when Alejandro and I mounted our horses, it was warm and we rolled up our sleeves and rode away from the body-guards. We played tag on horseback, and we called it "Cowboys and Indians." I rode Nabuco, a heavy, black, paso fino. Nabuco was the mother of at least six foals and colts, and there was a maternal manner to her. Alejandro rode Marlboro, a light-footed chestnut criollo, full of life; a bachelor, you could say. Marlboro bit and bucked, and I feared approaching him.

We galloped up mountains, *tac-a-tac, tac-a-tac,* the horses' hooves making music against the hard soil, and we were care-free. Atop the mountains, the horses halted, their panting was deep, and they were white with perspiration. They chewed their bits, eager and delighted, and under me, I felt Nabuco's body, awake, alive; she shivered. Below us, at the foot of the moun-tains, there was a reservoir. A pair of tiny birds, tinguas, flew low, dipping their wings in the water, refreshing themselves. Nearby, a family of Canadian geese south for the winter swam and plunged their heads in the water.

Once, Nabuco and I were winning a race against Marlboro and Alejandro—blazing through, *tac-a-tac-tac-a-tac,* eucalyp-tus branches scratching our faces and arms—until Nabuco and I tripped on the gravel pathway. Nabuco's chin bled while a pebble lay encrusted on my lip.

Bleeding, swallowing tears, I asked, "Did Martin Guerre spook Nabuco?" Martin Guerre was a donkey. He was angry and untamable. His hair was straggly, knotted with dirt. He was the hacienda's resident hobo, exploding from behind bushes when you were off guard.

Alejandro shook his head. He took his duties as big brother with great seriousness, and he said, "You were so fast! You beat me."

"I did?"

"Yes." It was his kindness.

"Stop. My lip hurts when I smile," I said.

On the lawn next to the house at Santa Nena, Alejandro and Angel trained for my brother's crew tryouts back in Canada. Angel took it to heart that his charge would make the team. They did bench presses, bench pulls, deadlifts, squat jumps, and arm curls. I joined them running, and they slowed the pace for my sake. They also played soccer and persuaded other bodyguards and workers to join their teams. Their cries of glee when someone scored and the high-fives that followed echoed across the mountains.

During Christmas breaks, Angel and I laid out a nativity scene that took up nearly the entire floor of Santa Nena's chapel. On Christmas eve, everyone who was in the hacienda— our family, the bodyguards, Tata, the caretakers and their families—was invited to the chapel, and we prayed the novena and sang villancicos.

In the afternoons, Angel taught me to drive, to switch gears and to pop the clutch quick enough to spin the Jeep into a donut.

The tires whirled in the clay. On the hills, he insisted that I hold the car with only the clutch, no brakes allowed. Such maneuvers, which he had mastered in bodyguard training, were skills he thought to pass along to Alejandro and me. In such ways, there was always a reminder of the violence beyond the high walls and gates. Of course, the holidays ended, and the biggest reminder was we had to board the plane by Labor Day for the first day of school in Canada.

Each summer that I returned from Canada, I had less in common with the country club teens whom I knew in Bogotá. In my silent ways, I judged them. They were a homogenous bunch, from the same schools, seemingly inbred. They were marked by a tribal dress code: girls and boys wore loafers complete with pennies, jeans with ironed creases, collared shirts, and sweaters draped over the shoulders with the sleeves tied across the chest. The boys' sweaters tended to be navy blue with a diamond design on the front. For boys, hair was always short, buzzed around the ear, military style. For girls, hair was long, their ears adorned with pearl studs.

In Toronto, I was used to cultural and racial diversity, which inspired creativity and personal expression. My hair was cut in a short bob, the latest trend from Vidal Sassoon. One day, my nails were glazed blue. I wore a white embroidered peasant blouse, a pink skirt, and pink cowboy boots. I was fifteen.

A girl approached me while I was in line in the cafeteria at the club. She had on riding jodhpurs, boots, and a starched-stiff white shirt. I admired her posture: shoulders erect, she stood tall. She exuded discipline—but also boredom.

Your hair makes you look like a lesbian, she said to me. Lesbians have butchy hair like yours.

My face reddened and my voice became shaky. Afterward I retreated into reading books. I talked in the voices of characters—*Kill the pig! Cut his throat! Bash him in!*—and Tata worried. She said reading was making me aloof, into a hermit destined to a quiet life on the sidelines. She reminded me to go outside. But, I told Tata, books were more interesting than the country club kids. Books brought me inside interesting places. *Shoot all the bluejays you want, if you can hit 'em, but remember it's a sin to kill a mockingbird.*

Afternoon tea with my grandmother was another distraction. Often, I found her lying on a divan, behind her the light of dusk glossing her garden. The gems on her fingers sparkled. Her bracelets jingled. Her wardrobe was couture—accentuating the waist, puffed sleeves, décolletés—in laces and silks, and trimmed with fur. It was in her library that I first encountered the work of Colette and Madame de Sévigné—and the image of my divan-lounging grandma, who had been brought up in Paris, embodied elements of that era. I knew my grandmother might think some scenes in those books were risqué for a teen, and by reflex, I stowed the books in my purse—though the vacancy left on the shelf was apparent. My grandmother concealed her smirk with a bite of a madeleine and a sip of Earl Grey. She likely thought that my French comprehension, taught in Toronto, was inadequate to understand certain scenes in their entirety. Perhaps, bless her, she recognized I was a kid asphyxiated behind the gates of our life in Bogotá.

You will do foolish things, but do them with enthusiasm.

I was sixteen years old, and a popular older boy—to my dismay, to my glee—asked me out to a disco. It was located in La Calera, on the city's outskirts, up through a dark road that divided the mountain and from where one could look down, as if by magic, upon Bogotá's shining lights.

"No, niña," Angel said. He said a drug trafficker, one that was sought after by the American Drug Enforcement Administration, had partied at the the disco the week prior. It was 1990.

"But, Angel, you don't understand what it means. This boy asked me out!" I said.

Bullocks to the rules! If there is a beast, we'll hunt it down! We'll close in and beat and beat and beat.

Angel was from Colombia's coastal region, and he had a congenial manner, which I was usually able to persuade to my side.

But he said, "Entiendo, niña. Pero no." He stroked his hand over his short corkscrew hair, as if in agony over hampering my tenuous social life. I had heard him and Tata discussing my solitude over coffee at the kitchen table.

The signs of drug money were displayed throughout Bogotá. The Colombians I knew were petrified that drug families and drug culture would penetrate our social spaces. That was why the grandmothers playing Canasta at the Country Club asked about kids' pedigree. Most of them had heard from DAS what drug traffickers were capable of.

While in Colombia, I have yet to go anywhere without at least one guard taking me in a bulletproof car. I could not go see Leonor at the government home without Juaquin, the bodyguard then assigned to me during the daylight hours. Juaquin was new to our family, and he was quiet, observant, and polite. He was small in height and borderline gaunt, though anyone could see he was all muscle. His two eyebrows, scrunched and creased, united as one, were not from anger, but rather offered the illusion that he was in deep thought, or agony, or both. His behavior around me was guarded, seemingly unsure of the protocol for our interactions. He opened and closed car doors. He did not address me unless I initiated the conversation.

But Juaquin's reserved demeanor towards me began evaporating the moment I asked him how he thought we should go about my visits to the halfway home.

It was a late morning in June 2001. We were standing outside my family's home in the north of the city. In a rare moment, the sky was clear of Bogotá's low hanging clouds, made famous in the paintings by Gonzalo Ariza, and we could see the mountain ranges that stood erect like walls around the city.

"Juaquin, if I show up with you," I said, "the conversation will shift to you—to why *I* need a bodyguard. They will ask me, Who are *you*? Why do *you* have a bulletproof car?"

Juaquin looked at me with a queer expression, in which astonishment was mixed with curiosity. Then, he said, "Está bien. This is how we will do it: when you are with them, you and I will pretend that we don't know each other."

"Agreed," I said to Juaquin. But my breath accelerated. I was a credulous twenty-seven-year-old, working through a recalcitrant fear of my homeland—a fear that was justified if we were to judge by what my reporting was uncovering. A professor from Columbia University, who heard me interviewed on National Public Radio, emailed me to be careful.

Juaquin asked, "Señorita, why do you want to do this?"

"Not sure," I said. "I know that taking me to meet these teens was not something you had expected in this job. I am sorry."

"No hay problema. I will help you," he said, smiling.

Like many of the bodyguards who passed through our household, Juaquin had been a government soldier. Months prior, he was part of an elite counter-guerrilla unit, trained under US supervision to fight the FARC, a job he'd held for nearly five years. There was a real possibility that Leonor and Juaquin could have encountered each other on the battlefields of southern Colombia's jungle. Juaquin had witnessed a handful of his army friends killed by the FARC, but he wasn't hardened, or at least not the way he could have been.

One afternoon while in the army, Juaquin was lifting corpses into body bags when he came upon a dead FARC girl; her scrawny body still in puberty. Her right breast was blown off and her hip was pulverized, and when Juaquin lifted her, her torso separated from her legs.

Fourteen soldiers from his squadron died that day. There were many more FARC casualties. The air held a blend of blood, gunpowder, and vomit.

"And after all that," I said, "and you're assigned to a crazy girl, who, of her own accord, looks for FARC tales."

"No, señorita, it's good what you're doing," Juaquin said. He was shy. His skin was still yellow with traces of the malaria, and he was skeletal. "If something happens, señorita, you run—make sure to first take your heels off!"

During those first weeks with Leonor, the war was intensifying. There were increased numbers of bodyguards around the kiosks by the entrance to the Country Club. Also, by the kiosks was an ambulance assigned to the First Lady. Juaquin said it was well equipped, even with what was necessary to transfuse blood. The First Lady was a family friend, a bond that dated back three generations. She was tall, slim, very blonde, and very attentive to fashion, having once worked PR in a couture house in Paris. Her looks were her brand, tight ball-gown-type dresses, chandelier earrings, custom-made suits in pastel colors with flower pins on lapels.

Juaquin's words churned in my mind: I pictured a wounded First Lady, her charred stiletto cast aside on the road.

"Señorita, the guys from the American Embassy, those guys have good armor," Juaquin said. The American Ambassador's bodyguards outside the club showed Juaquin their top-notch machine guns and walkie-talkies. Far superior than what he had to protect our family, Juaquin stressed. He sounded like a jealous kid talking about toys.

For weeks, my visits to Leonor's first halfway home were a secret between Juaquin and me. I didn't tell my family I was visiting former members of the FARC. If I told my parents, they would control my outings to try to keep me safe. They would say, "This isn't a game you're playing. What if you're kidnapped? What if you're caught in a crossfire?"

I knew enough to take further precautions. I asked Juaquin, "What bus comes near the halfway home?"

He relayed the different bus options, the traffic at various times of the day, the heavy construction on one certain route.

With this in mind in case the subject arose, I exited our family's car a few blocks away from Leonor's first government home, and I walked the rest of the way. Juaquin trailed me in the car, and he drove, very slowly, keeping less than half a block between us. He kept a machine gun under the passenger seat. This came to be our routine on days I visited Leonor. I felt rebellious and giddy, in a childlike way. Yet I had not forgotten that less than ten years prior, Alejandro had been a victim of a kidnapping.

CHAPTER SEVEN

Alejandro awoke again in the stuffy room, a room so tiny it fit only the queen-sized mattress he lay on. Black Mask and White Mask were cross-legged on the floor, at the foot of the bed, and each fidgeted with a machine gun. I pieced together such fragmentary details through the years, mainly by staying quiet and making myself invisible when the subject was brought up. The masks both wore jeans and black T-shirts. Black Mask was extremely skinny; he had a tattoo of a bouquet of black roses on his bicep, and from his wrists red amulets of the Virgin Mary hung. White Mask was on the fleshy side. Long dark hairs grew on his fingers. Evidently following an order, they did not address my brother except for the required "baño está aca" on the first day. Their cigarettes kept them behind a veil of smoke.

The boys stole sideways glances at Alejandro.

My brother repeated in his head: Padre Nuestro que estas en los cielos.[1]

White Mask was saying, hermano, there's more to life than your mamá's frijolada.

Black Mask responded, No jodas con mi mamá. He shook his machine gun, and for a moment, it looked like he'd use it to body-slam the fat kid. You like her beans. Puta, si que usted es un puta chancho, he said, laughter erupting. Black Mask handed White Mask the Walkman they shared. Su musica es pura mierda, he said.

Alejandro tensed hearing them disagree until he realized their tone was part of their friendship.

With each passing morning, it became easier to think about the abduction. On February 5, 1992, at eight-thirty in the morning, Alejandro sat at his desk, coffee in hand. The cleaning lady could be heard objecting, Señores, you are not authorized to come in. Señores! She appeared small next to the six men in military uniforms filing in. They flashed Uzis, AK-47s, and grenades. They ordered everyone against the wall and demanded to see ID's. Afraid, disoriented, Alejandro and his coworkers complied. A much older associate, who was known to have weak health, yelled, Who are you? Then, a muscled voice said, It's this short one, este es, and four of them were half-lifting, half-dragging Alejandro out the door.

Outside, six more men in military garb were waiting. A police car drove by without pausing. Alejandro, who's about five and a half feet tall, held onto an electricity post but two of the giants rifle-whipped him until he let go.[2] Once in the tiny room, the scar on his forehead began healing. He'd needed stitches, but only peroxide and paper towels were left for him on the mattress. Alejandro caught Black Mask nodding approval when he used it to clean the wound.

We'd been half-expecting a kidnapping since the days of M-19. The security specialists our family consulted had said not to keep a routine, and not to divulge on the phone where we planned to go. We grew up fearing the car that followed us. Once, an unknown driver who was parked on our street for too long prompted me to sleep with my street clothes on, and Alejandro taunted, "Loser, you let fear win."

Where had my brother's two bodyguards disappeared to? The bodyguards accompanied us everywhere. As a teen, Alejandro ran away from Angel, and Angel had to drive all over Bogotá looking for his car.

"Stupid," I'd said to Alejandro, though there had been a time when I had been willing to follow him, to run away together, and Angel cajoled us home.

Angel was not with him on the day he was abducted. Angel had retired from security and was driving a city bus. But the bodyguards with Alejandro on that day had worked with our family for over ten years, and in the loneliness of captivity, Alejandro could not accept that they'd been paid off. Later, it was said his bodyguards could have been involved though nothing was ever confirmed. For this reason, for some time, I hesitated to trust Juaquin.

The kidnappers appeared trained by Special Forces—the way they transferred him from car to car every few blocks, abandoning the white Mazda at the corner where the blue one was waiting.[3] The next stop they shoved him into a Renault, next into a Chevrolet.[4] They'd rehearsed the routes, studying the traffic at that time of the day. Within forty-five minutes, Alejandro was in the room with the mattress, being told to put on the dark green sweats. They still had the tags from the store. To put them on would be to accept being there, so he resisted.

Late in the afternoon of the first day, he took off his suit— jacket first, then pants. Careful to fold the pants at the creases, he told himself he would not be there for long. The masks were studying him already, so he made it quick—Alejandro rolled up his tie, an Hermès he'd charged on a credit card Mami provided for such purposes. "Buy what you need for your new job," she'd said. He tucked the tie into a pocket in his jacket. He removed his cufflinks, small silver studs, and slipped those, too, into the jacket pocket. A wing on his eyeglasses was broken. But he was glad he'd been too lazy that morning to insert contact lenses.

He didn't take off his watch, a gold Rolex given to him by Papi for graduating from business school. Not long before the abduction, Alejandro had arrived in Bogotá, after a year of lounging around Germany. He took a job in an engineering startup and was looking for an apartment.

White Mask escorted Alejandro to the toilet, his machine gun prodding, Hurry up.

Today was shower day, and Alejandro overheard one of the masks saying it was the first time in his life he'd had access to running water. Alejandro had found a toothbrush on the bed, and the bristles revealed it'd been used before.

Alejandro forced himself to have a routine. Mornings were for reading. Early on, he asked if he could have some books, and Black Mask, without uttering a word, provided a note pad for Alejandro to jot down the titles.

One afternoon when Alejandro awoke from a nap, he found *Don Quixote* lying by his head. Cervantes helped him survive. Alejandro's Dulcinea had long blond hair and cheeks like peaches, an image he summoned from a girl he dated in high school. He chose to forget that her hair's radiance came from a bottle, the complexion from a compact. Her popularity grew as she said "Yes, yes" to every boy. She and Alejandro had not been in touch for some time and she no longer meant anything to him, but he held her in his mind.

The security experts had said never to give out details about our family and friends, so when Alejandro put on the sweats, my brother made himself forget birthdays, club memberships, graduations, hobbies, favorite foods.

Padre Nuestro que estas en los cielos. Since we were toddlers, in Mami's arms, we prayed before bedtime. Even away at school, after a night of partying, Alejandro had repeated the supplications. There is a God in heaven, Don Quixote whispered, who does not neglect to punish evil and reward the good. And one of the sins that most offends God is ingratitude.

A lot was expected from Alejandro and he asked a lot from himself. A prep school and Ivy League education was intended to make him the next family patriarch. Already it was expected he would take control of our family's construction business.

The chill of the early morning mist said he had not been taken out of Bogotá.

It seems, Don Quixote said, that you are not versed in this kind of adventure; they are giants and if you are scared, get out of the way, and start your prayers elsewhere because I am going into battle against them.

Black Mask handed him lunch, watery lentils and sticky rice. Alejandro overheard the masks commenting about the relief that they were guaranteed food in this job. Alejandro learned to eat quickly or White Mask would announce that Alejandro was done and take the plate away so he could eat it himself.

Alejandro was unsure who did the cooking. It wasn't so bad, really, genuine peasant food, maybe a tad too salty.

At about the same time every day, one of the masks answered a knock on the door and received their plates from a woman. Once, she referred to Black Mask as "hijo mio." Black Mask always stood between her and the door, blocking Alejandro's view of her, protectively, almost lovingly. Thoughts about Black Mask and his mother discussing why they should agree to hide a hostage brought Alejandro to tears. His breath hurried, the back of his neck broke into a sweat. From the masks' slight hand-trembling, the sweat at *their* necks, trickling from under the masks, it was possible this was their first time guarding a hostage.

Agua? Alejandro asked.

Black Mask exited the room. He left the door open and the noise of soap operas on the radio filled the space. There was never a male voice in the background. Sometimes, there was the scent of incense and candles burning.

Black Mask returned with a glass of water. Whoever filled the glass had made the effort to include ice cubes. Gracias, Alejandro said. He was polite by nature.

White Mask imitated Alejandro saying thank you, and Alejandro's lips tensed up. One kick in the gut and this gordito will apologize. No, no, you will not lose your cool. Instead, Alejandro funneled the anger, the anxiety and the helplessness into rubbing the nail of the little finger on his right hand onto his thumb nail. His mind raced: You will safeguard your manners. The masks talked while they ate with their mouths open and it revolted Alejandro to see the chewed-up food. He recalled Mami saying, Napkin on the lap. Our grandmother trained the new houseboy, Serve from the left, take plates away from the right. Quickly, Alejandro diverted his thoughts: Don Quixote's niece and neighbors were right when they burnt all his novels about chivalry lest Don Quixote decided to personify a gentleman further.

White Mask was saying that Alejandro ate meat every day when he was home.

And what is that the rich drink? Whiskey? Black Mask brought an imaginary glass up to his lips, his pinkie stretching out. The masks laughed.

Alejandro would have welcomed some single malt, neat, please. He always liked single malt. If he closed his eyes, he could savor the pleasure of it; at the same time, the idea revolted him. He was kidnapped because people who gulped expensive liquor didn't care that boys like the masks didn't have food. He rubbed the fingernail on his index finger on the fingernail on his thumb. He hated these boys. Their bodies stank, their feet stank, their mouths reeked.

Afternoons were for exercising for at least two hours. Squats, lunges, push-ups, all around the mattress, while the masks gaped. Release the anger, the humiliation. Neither Black Mask nor White Mask would see tears. Alejandro plotted to end his life. But no razors. No cords. No shower curtain. Maybe there was a way to use the sweatpants. Dearest God, you have abandoned me.

No. No. One more set of squats, lunges, push-ups, sit-ups, star-jumps, push aside the thoughts of suicide. God, you are testing me. Bring on exhaustion so sleep comes more easily tonight. Dios mio, por fa, just *one* hour of restful sleep. The sweat ran down Alejandro's back and for a moment he laughed, and the masks, taken by surprise, clutched their guns. Something inside Alejandro awoke—he had power, after all; his soul was flourishing in this misery. He could have hugged the masks. He was going to be OK. Or was this madness?

The sunset meant it was time for watching television. All three squeezed onto the mattress, and Alejandro, much shorter than the two, lay in the middle, elbows bent and cupped hands holding his head. The position of the three on the bed was a habit now. The guns, idling on the edge of the mattress, framed the three. Up close, the boys smelled of fried food and sweat. Alejandro, too, stank and who cared.

Alejandro didn't know when, exactly, the Rolex went missing from his wrist. Three or four days earlier; maybe a week? In his mind, he turned over the right words to ask about it.

The masks lost themselves in the world of teens in a Beverly Hills high school. It revealed their lust for fast cars, club scenes, the beach, girls in bikinis, cell phones, and stylish clothes. Alejandro felt Black Mask analyzing him more than usual. It made Alejandro's cheeks burn.

In his thoughts, he picked apart the behavior of people from the Country Club and from our neighborhood: their chauffeurs halted their level-4 bulletproof cars in the middle of shopping intersections, one bodyguard bolted to the corner, another opened the asshole's door. Cars honked—nothing mattered because the asshole thought he was akin to a Hollywood actor.

In the years to come, Alejandro drove his own car and opted for underground parking to downplay the parade of bodyguards who followed him in another car. When he went shopping or to restaurants, he instructed them to stay at least a half block away.

Less than a month after Alejandro's abduction, in early March, Stu was sent by the kidnapping insurance company in London. Stu was a tall, loud-mouthed Londoner who traveled the globe negotiating ransoms. From my father's study, he recorded all phone calls our household received. Stu did not speak Spanish, and my father stayed by his side. My mother sent them tea and biscuits.

A letter from my mother came in the mail for me at boarding school. She explained that Stu believed there could be a proof of life sent to me, to my school P.O. box.

For Alejandro, weeks in captivity passed. At night after the TV shows ended and the set was off, Alejandro crossed his arms over his chest and closed his eyes. Alarmed, he opened them again and he felt a shadow, like a vampire over him. By reflex, he lifted his hands to cover his face. The masks slept, their bodies stamped against the cold tile floor at the foot of the mattress. You must keep the schedule, he told himself. He was not sure when he fell asleep, or if he did indeed sleep. The prayer had its own engine: Padre Nuestro que estas en los cielos. The light bulb above the mattress remained lit.

My father, at home in his study with Stu, waited for the phone call that did not come when the male caller had said it would. Papi's belly rounded, his shoulders humped, layers of wrinkles appeared under his eyes. The stress led to his diabetes.

My mother, too, counted the days that he'd been missing—nearly one hundred. Two of her teeth rotted and her hair fell out. Every week, she made the pilgrimage to the church of The Divine Child.

I haggled with God: Alejandro's life in exchange for never smoking another cigarette; Alejandro's life in exchange for joining a nunnery. Final papers and exams were nearing before school let out for spring vacation, and books made the days go by faster. Nothing connected to Alejandro ever arrived in the mail.

In May, the male caller told Stu (and my father who stood nearby) that a proof of life was going to be left in a bin in a restroom in a mall. Angel, the trusted bodyguard, was sent to retrieve it. Angel found a tape wrapped in newspaper. It played my brother's voice, reading that day's newspaper headlines. The voice lacked expression. For several days then, Rosa Milagrosa, a statue of a virgin, resided in my parents' bedroom. Rosa Milagrosa was circulated around the families of hostages, and many said they'd received good news while she visited their home.

Alejandro was running in place, barefoot. He didn't care if the masks gaped at him. He spoke to the masks because that was what the kidnapped did to avoid conversing with imaginary friends: Running feels good, he screamed, delight in his face. Sweat trickled down his chest, back and forehead.

Black Mask addressed Alejandro, We were thinking—his amulets twinkled from the light bulb above—we want to exercise with you. At first, Alejandro mistook his tone for an order, then, because those were the first non-essential words uttered to him, he said, Sure. The masks put their guns in the bathroom.

The boys followed Alejandro's lead: crunches, star jumps, push-ups. Sprinting on the spot, fast! End with jumping jacks. It was the rowing workout from boarding school.

During his captivity, he recalled the camaraderie developed in exercising, first with Angel, then with his high school crew team. They sat in the cafeteria together for spaghetti and steak dinners, and they shaved their heads.

White Mask had a hard time doing push-ups. Señor, am I doing it right? he asked.

What? Alejandro asked. Señor?

The masks giggled at one another. Black Mask said, We don't know your name, señor. Black Mask brought his hand up to his mouth, shy, nervous.

Okay, Alejandro said. He might have meant, okay that you don't know my name. Or, okay, you have the right push-up technique. He himself hardly knew which.

Alejandro began looking forward to the afternoon exercise. White Mask's pants grew baggy while he and Black Mask took on the appearance of light-weight athletes. The masks cut back on their cigarettes. The odor of smoke began fading from the room.

It was with shame that Alejandro recalled the taunt his prep school team chanted to the public-school boys who beat them, "That's alright, that's okay, you'll work for us some day."

90210 was on again. The TV flashed fancy restaurants, fast cars, yachts, and ski holidays. There was never any rain or thunderstorms.

White Mask addressed Alejandro, Señor, those people live like that in real life?

Alejandro remembered the way the gears transitioned, ever so smoothly, in the Porsche he drove in college. Don't know, he told the masks.

The masks forgot to turn the TV off and Alejandro half-listened to the ten o'clock news.

The year was 1992. The Medellín Cartel and Pablo Escobar were carrying out select kidnappings to push President César Gaviria not to sign any extradition papers that would make drug traffickers face trials in the US. The drug lords said they preferred a tomb in Colombia than a jail cell in America.

Black Mask slipped out for a moment and returned with a roll of Scotch tape.[5] Mamá thinks you can fix them, your glasses.

White Mask asked, You want to play cards with us?

Okay, Alejandro said.

They settled around the mattress. Alejandro found it easy to read the masks' cards depending on their body language, but he let them win.

His mind was on the news; for two generations now, since our grandfather was the mayor of Bogotá, no one close to us was involved in politics. Our grandfather had been dead for thirteen years. His kidnapping was not political. Much later, we found out his kidnappers were part of a gang of common criminals out to make quick cash.

Four months after his abduction, in June, my parents placed a half-page advertisement at the bottom of the newspaper, *El Tiempo*'s, front page. It read, "Spencer tennis balls have arrived in Colombia. Just like the ones used at Wimbledon." They used the name Spencer, after my brother's roommate in boarding school, and with that, Alejandro was supposed to understand that Stu was in Colombia and the negotiation was happening. But Alejandro never saw the ad.

White Mask asked, What is that place the Country Club like?

Alejandro's face didn't betray emotion. "El Country" was where as a teen he played tennis. The club was an oasis amid the crowded buses of la Carrera Quince, farting dark clouds, and the homeless children drinking gasoline and blowing fireballs and begging for spare change. Then, you show your membership ID at the gate, and suddenly, flowers greet you, sprinklers tend to manicured lawns, and Stepford wives in white T-shirts and white miniskirts strut along in a fog of perfume.

Umm, snobs, mostly, Alejandro said. Once the words were out, he believed the people there were snobs. He hated the incestuous crowd he'd known since the playground. There was the guy who took over as newspaper publisher when his grandfather retired, and the guy who was groomed to become a minister like his father. And along came the guy who repeated his last name as if he were royalty. He dropped French and English words into the conversation, and the words were often mispronounced and misused. Losers, really, Alejandro added. Alejandro was beginning to think of leaving behind all he possessed. Don Quixote again. From that moment and to this day, Alejandro would support candidates who pursued market-friendly policies. Jobs, he'd say, people need jobs.

Black Mask dealt the cards. You can take us to the Country Club one day, señor. Give us some whiskacho, he said. He turned to White Mask, Chancho, he takes you there, you'll puta eat all the food at that club.

Alejandro gathered it was Sundays when the older man came. El Viejo did not try to disguise himself; he was a decade past middle age, not too tall. His black mustache was professionally trimmed and his white hair was razed military style. He had olive skin. From the way he asked the masks about Alejandro's health and diet and spirits, he was the boss. Alejandro regarded his visits as a sign he had not been forgotten.

One Sunday, the old guy addressed Alejandro. Your father is a stubborn man, he said. El Viejo took out a pistol from his jeans. He continued, Your father thinks this is another business deal. From the guarded words my father spoke on the telephone, the old man sensed there was a professional advisor, and Stu's presence was a threat to him.

The old man was passing his pistol from hand to hand, and Alejandro wanted to vomit; he lost awareness of what happened next. Padre Nuestro que estas en los cielos.

The fear that you have, whispered Don Quixote, makes you neither see nor hear right.

A purple light fell over the room, followed by sparkles. White Mask was standing with his back to them. Black Mask had a yellow shadow behind him.

The old man did not hit Alejandro with the gun, and instead tucked it back in his pants. The pistol was only for intimidation. His black leather army boots were worn-in and polished beyond shine.

There's no reason to pay attention to these things, said Don Quixote. There's no reason to be angry. They are invisible, and we won't take revenge on anyone.

Alejandro sank into a feeling of abandonment. He didn't know Mami and Papi well. When he was fourteen, he'd been deposited in boarding school in Canada, and before that, he'd been attended by nannies and drivers and bodyguards who led him from school to after-school activities to dinner to bed.

Black Mask was handing him a glass of water, urging him to drink. Black Mask was saying, El Viejo also treats us like we are disposable. He cannot kill you. It would kill the deal.

White Mask urged Alejandro to sit, watch TV with them. White Mask looked nervous. A soccer game was on and there was about to be a penalty shot.

El Viejo is going to travel. He won't be back for two weeks at least, said Black Mask.

Don't tell him that, said White Mask.

How can it matter?

He can't know shit like that.

Alejandro accepted a cigarette.

Black Mask said he attended church whenever he could, always receiving the Holy Communion. Black Mask believed in the afterlife when he was going to be rewarded.

What about confession? Alejandro asked him.

What about it? Black Mask responded. They were playing cards again.

Surely you cannot believe holding me here is not a sin.

Black Mask told Alejandro that his mother confessed to the priest. The priest forgave them. The priest told her it was justice for the poor.

Don Quixote nudged Alejandro, It's not for you to go begging judgments from philosophers, advice from the Holy Book, fables from poets, rhetorical prayers, miracles from saints ... Shut up! Alejandro thought. You're a silly character, invented by a writer who was bored while in prison.

Black Mask shuffled the cards, and as Alejandro took in Black Mask's bony fingers, he imagined poverty, swollen bellies, lifetimes of malaria, of cholera. Of mothers and babies dying at childbirth. The Joker slipped from the deck. Not far from the Country Club, families built homes from stolen billboards and torn tarps. It came to Alejandro that you could pray, but it wouldn't do much good. Two years later, at a relative's wake, Alejandro stood with crossed arms, clenched jaw, and judging eyes while the rest of us chorused a Hail Mary.

After two months, the masks relaxed at shower time. Alejandro's hair and beard were longer than any adventurer's.

The cards ready? Alejandro asked. His quads ached from the daily exercise.

The masks turned to face him, and the mood was grim. A change was coming.

Alejandro's suit had disappeared the first afternoon, and now it lay on the mattress. Tears flooded Alejandro's eyes. He sat down on the mattress. The suit still held the residue of his cologne, of home!

Alejandro studied White Mask. Yes, White Mask confirmed.

The two looked so different from the first time Alejandro laid eyes on them. The three had constructed a triangle of cohabitation.

In the suit pocket, Alejandro found the watch. It sparkled. Alejandro adjusted his shirt collar over his jacket, and placed the watch on the mattress. The door was open and he walked out of the room without looking back at the masks. Two men he'd never seen before drove him to an intersection. From there my brother hailed a cab. He was home within an hour.

Everyone saw the shift in Alejandro's character after the kidnapping. He closed himself off to us. He passed much time in silence, eyebrows furrowed, staring at the air in front of him, and rubbing the fingernail stub that remained on his thumb. A glaze resided over his eyes. When he did speak, he referenced death and was mean-spirited. Anger brewed inside him, and to witness my brother's pain caused me sorrow. I sensed he could not surpass the misfortunes explicit in the lives of Black Mask and White Mask.

Leonor could have easily been one of my brother's captors. In her, I was looking for clues to what Black Mask and White Mask might have been like, and what kind of relationship Alejandro might have developed with them. How had he survived this ordeal? If it happened to my brother, it could happen to me. By 2000, every three hours someone was kidnapped somewhere in Colombia.[6] This meant that more than half the world's kidnappings were taking place in Colombia. Between 1970 and 2013, 39,058 people were kidnapped.[7] Many cases were not reported for fear of retribution from the captors.

So: If I were to be kidnapped, how would I take this negative experience and turn it into a positive? If I could understand the captors' motives, such an experience might pass from the realm of the frightening to the pragmatic.

My feelings were confused. I was fond of Leonor, and I held such respect for her resilience. I was in awe of all she still faced ahead of her. Leonor had not victimized my family, but I assumed her membership in the FARC meant she had victimized other Colombians. FARC was the biggest culprits of kidnappings. According to the Center for Historical Memory, of a sample of 9,082 cases of kidnappings, thirty-seven percent were kidnapped by the FARC, thirty percent by another illegally armed group, the ELN (the National Liberation Army), twenty percent by criminal networks, four percent by paramilitaries, and nine percent by others.[8] It was why Alejandro did not want me risking my safety by spending long hours with former FARC.

I had stopped regarding Leonor with the label of "former FARC." She was a young woman conditioned by her environment, and her behavior was a response to the pulse of her hometown and the challenges her family withstood.

CHAPTER EIGHT

Oliverio refused to leave Los Azules, but Mercedes moved with the children to Mocoa, around 1995. Shortly after they arrived, Mercedes gave birth to Sergio and Luis. Leonor was soon turning eleven years old, and she mothered the boys like Consuelo had tended to her and Leo. She found life worthwhile when Sergio and Luis nudged up at her breast and closed their eyes.

Those first years in Mocoa, Leonor saw less and less of Leo and Consuelo. It seemed the two of them were always busy, having been invited somewhere by one new friend or another. The town life of Mocoa was opening up not only the teens' social lives but also their tastes and habits. Leo began following bands on the radio and lip-syncing to songs. But the biggest difference was that for Consuelo, her appearance became important. Strewn about the house were Consuelo's dresses, and Leonor tried them on. She also experimented with her sister's make-up. When Consuelo returned home in the early evenings and the two girls sat down, Consuelo described meeting up with boys and men, and there was intensity and passion in Consuelo's voice.

She and Leo stayed away from home a lot, wary of the tension between adults. Mercedes, formerly relegated to the duties of a stay-at-home mother when they had lived on the farms, became the breadwinner now that Oliverio had stayed behind in Los Azules. At times, Abuelita traveled from the countryside to tend to the children, but she was frightened by the town's electricity, traffic, and noise, and she stayed inside praying. Leonor sat near while the twins climbed onto her lap, and Abuelita's bony hands blessed them with the sign of the cross. Abuelita whispered Psalm Ninety-One—"... Whoever dwells in the shelter of the Most High will rest in the shadow of the Almighty."

Milton took week-long trips away from town. He discovered that there was money working as a drug mule for a small-time drug runner. He swallowed pellets filled with processed cocaine and then travelled by bus from city to city. He defecated these pellets, washed them, and delivered them.

Upon his return, he handed Mercedes lumps of cash. Mercedes held her breath while counting the money, and after she was done, she relaxed. She did not ask her son where he had been or with whom. She seemed to not be concerned that he was changing, at times acting arrogant and impudent. Often, Mercedes could not scrimp enough to get by, and she relied on Milton and not Oliverio.

Now and then, Oliverio made the journey to see the family in Mocoa. (Los Azules from Mocoa was only about a two-day-walk.) With the plans for his farm destroyed, and lonesome without Mercedes, he drank more. His body shriveled, and he made little sense when he spoke. When a drunk Oliverio crossed the threshold, the children knew to vacate the home. Now a defiant Leonor stayed. Within minutes, Oliverio cornered her. She stood still. A wave of dizziness and despair circulated inside her. His glazed breath felt warm on her. His mouth shaped words, but she tuned him out and did not hear him. He raped her.

Days later, once Oliverio departed for Los Azules, Leonor told Mercedes what Oliverio had done. The mother called the daughter a liar. Mercedes yanked the electrical cords from the wall and chased Leonor around the house, jumping over furniture, whipping at her with the chords. Mercedes screamed that—without a doubt, she said—Leonor had tempted Oliverio as she pranced around in Consuelo's skimpy outfits.

Mercedes finally caught Leonor and held her down to whip her. Sergio and Luis, toddlers, watched and cried. Mercedes didn't stop until Leonor's leg was bleeding. From the beating, Leonor developed a scar, and for years, whenever her leg cramped and ached, she cursed her mother.

Consuelo, who had vowed to look after Leonor, wasn't around. There were times when Consuelo, like Milton, wasn't home for days. And Leo had no time for Leonor, his friends knocking on the door early in the mornings, rushing him outside. He didn't invite Leonor to come along. But the day of the beating, Sergio reached out his arms, asking to be picked up and when Leonor did, he embraced her. He wiped her tears, and Leonor found solace.

"After that, Mamá said I could no longer live under her roof, but I was a child," she told me. We were on the phone, and I could hear Dahlia's giggles. Dahlia, a tot, sat on Leonor's lap enjoying a snack.

After Mercedes whipped her, Leonor lost track of the number of nights that she slept on the street. Having learnt the lesson from her father's behavior, Leonor dressed like a boy, and she believed it was insurance against men touching her. But by her dainty hands and her walk, and by her small waist (and perhaps she already possessed that habit of hers, of coquettishly swaying her shoulders) it was easy to tell, even by her voice, that here was a beautiful girl.

On the street, Leonor met Redhead. He was a boy her age—she called him "el pelirojo," because he had paprika-like freckles sprinkled on his cheeks and hair like the head of a matchstick. To know that Redhead—though lanky and feeble—kept a piece of a broken bottle within his grasp consoled Leonor. She was sure he would protect her, and so she followed his lead, and they squatted inside deserted buildings. With him securing the space, she was able to give in to slumber for a few hours.

Some days, Leonor and Redhead sold slices of watermelon at streetlights. They were employed by an old woman who had approached them. But Leonor was often starved and she devoured the watermelon, its juices jetting down her chin and arms. The woman slapped Leonor when she came back without money, and so Leonor went car to car, begging drivers for pocket change. Most cars were scraps of tin, spewing dark smoke. Once or twice, a luxury car, overdone with tinted windows, shiny hubcaps, and immense headlights, circled the neighborhood. As Leonor approached the cars, the drivers rolled up the windows. She stood by the car windows, and the drivers looked elsewhere or pretended to fiddle with the radio. She caught glimpses of her reflection on the cars' sideview mirrors, and she was repulsed by her tattered clothes and soiled face.

Redhead was shrewd, and one day, he returned with plates loaded with mountains of rice and arepas. By word of mouth, he discovered they would be offered food if they showed up at FARC camps located in Mocoa's jungle periphery. Feeling faint, aware she could not go another day without food, Leonor ventured into FARC camps to be fed. She accepted seconds of rice, beans, and lentils, and soon, she helped herself to them. She became a regular at the encampments, and she began thinking of FARC members as friends and allies, compassionate to her situation. A FARC nurse disinfected the wound on her leg, from her mother's beating, and covered it with bandages after white pus oozed from it.

Some nights, Leonor lingered by the fire in the middle of camp while someone strummed a guitar and others sang. It was then she was able to sleep uninterrupted, without worrying whether Redhead and his broken glass were watching over her.

Members of the FARC intermingled with the daily life of her town and of the entire area, and many of them were people she knew. Some locals wore FARC fatigues, others didn't—but nearly all of Mocoa's residents were sympathetic to the group's Communist roots. For Leonor and for many teens in Colombia's southern communities, the FARC camps offered diversions. There was booze, and sometimes there was dancing, and there was also the thrill of being allowed to handle a gun. The camps were akin to a right of passage, a way to rebel against parents.

Mercedes kept the door of their home locked. When Leonor strolled by, Sergio rushed to the window and waved kisses at his sister. One afternoon, Leonor stumbled on her hairbrush on the curb outside their home, which Sergio had placed there for her. He was aware of his sister's obsession with her looks, having watched her try on every dress that Consuelo brought home.

Leonor considered how she must look to Sergio, and so every few days, she walked to the river to wash herself and detangle her hair. She was thankful for the river since around this time she began menstruating.

Niña, ven aca. A man on a motorcycle called her over one sweltering morning while she was standing around at the side of the road holding pieces of watermelon. He offered to pay Leonor two thousand pesos (roughly two dollars) to clean his house.

Leonor agreed, of course, and she mounted on the motorbike behind him. He slid through traffic, past the horse-drawn carriages, the trucks, the outdoor market. They went some distance outside Mocoa, past where she knew was the crossing that led to the FARC camps, onto a dirt road looking down over vast pastures. They sped on, along sharp curves and over dangerous embankments. It was far enough away from town that it was desolate.

She asked where they were going, her voice cracking. The wind blew and she repeated the question.

He didn't answer. What was happening?

Leonor panicked. She threw herself off the motorcycle and landed on her shoulder. The man didn't slow down. He disappeared behind the bike's fumes. Leonor's shoulder throbbed.

She walked back to town. She returned to eating watermelons and begging for change, and showing up for meals at nearby FARC camps.

Some time later, someone driving an opulent car—with the tinted windows down and music blaring—tracked down the watermelon woman and asked to buy Leonor's virginity. The offer came from Mocoa's most powerful drug trafficker—"El Patrón" was how Leonor referred to him. "El Patrón bought what he wanted," Leonor told me. She alluded to an abundance of money from smuggling illicit drugs. Among such men, it was a status symbol to boast about sleeping with virgins, and the watermelon woman assured his go-between that Leonor was undeniably a virgin. Why wouldn't she be?

In the following days, the old woman softened towards Leonor. I want to help you, she said, a forced heartiness to her voice. The sudden goodwill was the conduct of someone with a motive, and this was not lost on Leonor. Her mother's behavior and the months spent on the streets had hardened Leonor.

What is it? she asked the watermelon woman.

The old woman divulged the offer from El Patrón. Leaning in closer to Leonor as if they were longtime chums, trying to win her over with eye contact, the old woman said they would divide the money, 20 million pesos, about US$9,000 dollars. This was real money, able to change both of their lives, the woman said. She gave Leonor a smile meant to charm, to sway her towards agreeing.

No, Leonor said. It was the answer of a girl who at that moment figured out she held the upper hand.

The mafioso's proposition made Leonor understand that she was beautiful—and by all means, this was her asset. Her blossoming good looks—skin like tanned porcelain, ample hair, a youthful body—was her key to surviving. Despite being homeless, and despite wearing rags, she had control over men who lusted after her, and powerful men at that. It was possible that the man on the motorcycle tried to abduct her in order to bring her to the drug trafficker.

To be compensated for sex was perhaps the most accessible "job" for women in those drug-growing areas. Prostitutes at times collected payment in coca leaves which they then sold. In her hometown, prostitution was one of the scant means that a woman might attain financial independence. Leonor's circumstances would lead her towards a variation of this occupation.

CHAPTER NINE

Some nights Leonor slept in the FARC camps, and other nights she slept on Mocoa's streets. But occasionally she missed her siblings and she came home, and Mercedes allowed it. One Saturday evening, Leonor studied her older sister preening herself for a night out. Leonor was twelve, Consuelo sixteen. First, Consuelo painted her fingernails blood-red. She'd saved money to buy the nail polish because she wanted to look sophisticated. They sat on a mattress, its springs exposed.

Consuelo told her younger sister that men from the FARC were more passionate lovers than the timid city soldiers.[1] City soldiers were frightened that country women would use black magic to enchant them to fall in love with them. As if I know black magic, Consuelo was saying.

Consuelo was boy crazy, and several young men regularly doted on her.

Consuelo first became obsessed with how on TV lovers unleashed their scripted flame for one another. Late one night, under the covers, Consuelo told Leonor she liked a scruffy and muscular macho hombre. You're gross, was Leonor's reply.

Consuelo described to her little sister how she imagined it would be: Her breasts, swollen though tender. His legs, lean and defined from outdoor work. His broad back from weeding with a steel hoe. Their sweat. Stop it, Consuelo, Leonor insisted, and the older sister laughed.

That Saturday evening, Consuelo was putting on sheer pantyhose, and Leonor reached out to feel the shiny nylon.

Leonor tried on Consuelo's high heels. They fit her. The older sister slipped on a black dress. No one in the family asked Consuelo how she could have afforded to buy the new outfit, or if someone had given it to her as a gift.

Consuelo had bleached her hair a blonde that was almost white, and her reflection in the mirror stunned her. I don't look like myself, Consuelo remarked. It was the first time that Leonor became aware of the power of fashion and clothes in putting out an image to the world.

Consuelo wanted to move to Neiva or Cucuta, anywhere where there was more nightlife and action. Consuelo squirted on a little patchouli—she wanted to save what was left in the bottle—but, at the last minute, she sprayed some on her neck, too.

You look beautiful, Leonor said to her.

Outside, the noise of Mocoa—cars honking, music blaring from the cars—palpitated. It was time to be alive.

The loud music disturbed Mercedes's twins. Leonor was giving Sergio and Luis the last bottle of the day. She referred to them as "my twins."

Two days later, when Leonor was caring for Sergio and Luis, Consuelo was still missing. A crowd outside their home prompted Leonor to cage the boys in their crib and skip out to investigate.

Dios mio, a woman muttered.

Consuelo's corpse was in the street. Blood threaded out from her cracked skull. Her body had been thrown from a passing truck.

It was a green truck, said a boy. I saw it. His mother hushed him. For him to be a snitch would be a death sentence.

Leonor was going to vomit. Consuelo's nails were still painted red. Pins stuck from her left eye.[2] Her right eye was missing. She was muddy. Her thighs were bruised. Around her ankles, marks and blood showed where she'd been tied with barbed wire.

What a shame that beautiful dress is ruined, someone said.

Someone else pointed out she was not wearing underwear.[3]

Whose dogs are those? Who can stop them?

Everyone knew Consuelo was Leonor's sister, yet, no one offered comfort. The pavement seemed to be slipping away under her.

Some hours later, Leo put his arm around Leonor and led her home. She could not stop shivering. "But I did not cry," Leonor told me.

That night, after Leo was sleeping beside her, the warmth of his body a comfort, Leonor sprang up and grabbed the nail polish and painted red each of her fingernails and toenails. She blew on them until they were dry and then hid the polish under the mattress.

With Oliverio in Los Azules, Milton took charge. After he moved Consuelo's corpse to forensics, an unpronounced agony sedated the family. There followed shock, disbelief, denial, and for Milton, a longing for vengeance. For weeks, Mercedes remained too frail to get out of bed. Leonor was again left to tend for herself, and continued to spend much of her time outside the family's home, sleeping on the streets and frequenting FARC camps for food.

I didn't understand why a seemingly innocent young woman would be murdered, and I told Juaquin what Leonor had described. Juaquin said, "Look, señorita, that girl who was murdered, how can I tell you?" He paused and decided it'd be okay to clear his mind: "She was a puta, sleeping around with men from different armed groups." Consuelo was clearly a slut because girls like her, who passed on intelligence to the FARC, were dangerous, and were the reason Juaquin's soldier friends were shot or kidnapped. That was the message from her killers— Stop snitching.

Leonor recalled Consuelo associated with men from different armed groups, consorting with government soldiers and men from the FARC.[4] Unknowingly, Consuelo revealed information about one side to the other.[5] At first Leonor told me she wasn't sure who killed Consuelo. Years later, Leonor felt uninhibited enough to reveal government soldiers—part of a counter-guerrilla unit like Juaquin's—were responsible.[6]

Consuelo didn't have proper ID, and government soldiers considered anyone without government-issued paperwork to be a guerrilla. Of all the children, only Sergio and Luis, who were born in Mocoa, were registered and given government-issued identities.[7]

The cadence of Leonor's speech marked her as having grown up in southern Colombia, in FARC-country, and while she was in the cities after she demobilized from FARC, authorities narrowed in on her and asked to see her government-issued ID. As a demobilized FARC, she had another type of ID, and authorities often detained her and called the government's rehabilitation office to vouch that her criminal record was clear. Leonor would continue to face this sort of discrimination, regardless of—or perhaps even as a rebuke to—the FARC-government peace accord of 2016.

Juaquin told me of a video shown to soldiers during the early days of military training in which the FARC bragged about using pretty girls as a trap.[8] The video was filmed by the FARC themselves and hastily left behind in a camp the army attacked. When Juaquin saw Leonor, the warning from his captain came to his mind: "Beautiful girls are the FARC's spy whores," the captain had said and pointed to body bags. "Fuck a FARC whore and that's how you'll come home to your mother, in a body bag."

CHAPTER TEN

Juaquin's group, all forty-five men, especially the captain and three sergeants, comprised an elite anti-guerrilla squad. They were hand-picked by the Colombian Special Forces, who were trained by Americans. This meant that Juaquin was a "professional soldier," and he spent much time in regions where Leonor's group, the 41st Front of the FARC's Southern Bloc, held control.

He heard tales of soldiers who unearthed caches of money and disappeared to lead the lifestyles of the rich. Jorge, another counter-guerrilla soldier, had said, in half-joke but with wide eyes, that they needed to look out for where the soil appeared uneven.

That's where those hijueputas buried the drug money, hermano, Jorge told Juaquin. They were not unlike those in Leonor's group who also desired to amass wealth—and to afford sports cars, SUVs with tinted windows and neon headlights, and breast augmentations for their women.

But Juaquin—when in areas controlled by the FARC, in Caquetá, Putumayo, and Guaviare departments—worried more about stepping on land mines.

As they did on most days, the squadron hiked, for extended periods of fourteen hours or more, in the heat and humidity.[1] *Slap, slap-woosh* echoed the blows of the soldiers' machetes, as they hacked a path through overgrown grass and weeds. The sun was fiery, and the air was stagnant and oppressive. Juaquin's shirt clung to his skin. He hauled five hundred cartridges pasted like magnets around his torso.

In the distance, on the mountain tops, there grew majestically tall and thick trees—mahogany and oak. The sun had turned their leaves yellow. There was no sign of rain.

The scratched up 762 rifle dangled over Juaquin's shoulder.

Jorge said, Be careful, hermano, that junk yard shit will jam and *pow!* get you killed.

It was in Juaquin's character not to reply, but he cursed Jorge and the mosquitoes.

He knew when his squadron entered what army intelligence considered a FARC red zone because coca plants were even more bountiful, flourishing mile after mile. What would have passed for an abandoned shed with broken windows and patched-up walls was a cocaine-processing lab. They marched further. Poppy flowers in bloom upholstered the fields in red velvet, and when the wind blew, the fields were flecked with crimson spots, like bloodstains.

The captain radioed in the location. He said they would return this way, and flick a match and watch the flames.

"La Candileja," Juaquin thought. Locals in this region were bound to say that a great fire was the ghost of an old woman, who (so the legend said) was burnt alive inside her shed, alongside her sons. It was said the murder happened in the 1940s, a decade when political violence took root, and the FARC's Sureshot first organized self-defense groups. Juaquin had heard farmers vow that neither shamans nor prayers nor Holy Water appeased her rage, and so "La Candileja" turned onto forests and crops for revenge.

The first time that Juaquin felt death courting him was the afternoon the FARC attacked Miraflores, a military base in remote southeastern Guaviare department. It was August 3, 1998. Juaquin and his squadron were about twelve miles away from Miraflores, but such was the echo of explosions and shots, that it gave the impression it was mere blocks away. They radioed in, and a sergeant's fright spat out from the walkie-talkie: The hijueputa guerrilleros are like ants.

Send the support planes, the sergeant said. Static broke up his voice.

But there were overcast skies and the planes could not land.[2]

Through the walkie-talkie, Juaquin heard explosions blasting the base. It was the sound of artisan bombs made from gas cylinders, which was FARC's secret weapon.[3] The FARC emptied the gas out of a tank normally used in a household stove, and they filled it with metal, nails, wrenches, pieces of iron, explosives, and feces.

From beyond there came the sharp roar of thunder, and there was a sudden freshness in the air. It rained most of the night, and a thick ribbon of the Colombian flag, the yellow, blue and red, was the only way to tell guerrillas from soldiers.[4]

Juaquin was still a distance away, and it was hard for him to breathe. The rain and the wind raced over the hills and the bush, and swept particles of gunpowder and dust clouds. The smell of smoke seeped into Juaquin's clothing, and his hair and his skin.

During the first hours, the FARC surrounded most of the government authorities in the area.[5] Nearly eight hundred guerrillas closed in, possibly two thousand more provided support. The FARC had planned every detail: Prior to the attack, they ordered two hundred roasted hens from a local restaurant, as part of the supplies they needed to sustain the combat.[6]

Miraflores was the largest anti-narcotics base in the country. More than sixty percent of the cocaine produced and exported from Colombia, most of which was consumed in the US, originated in the region that surrounded Miraflores.[7] The base was ground zero for operations launched by the American Drug Enforcement Administration. The DEA operated by contracting private counterinsurgency trainers and intelligence agents, who worked together with the Colombian police and the Colombian army.[8] Juaquin's was one of a handful of counter-guerrilla units operating out of Miraflores who provided support to the DEA, though they were not contracted by the Americans.

The attack that day was one of the deadliest in Colombia's history. By destroying Miraflores, the FARC intended to consolidate complete power over the region and show their strength to the Americans. The FARC already controlled 50,000 acres of coca fields.[9]

Juaquin and the rest of the elite soldiers—through rain and thunder, under a black sky that breathed fire—built trenches, right where they were. Juaquin was determined to stay calm. Through the night, he strained to see in the distance. After twenty hours of waiting, Juaquin and the others took a chance and emerged from the trench.[10] It was past noon of the next day. The battle had ended, and there remained the cleaning up.

That evening, twenty-six hours after the initial shots on Miraflores were fired, the army helicopter collected the dead. The chopper was on its fifth trip, and Juaquin helped to unload the corpses. An estimated one hundred and twenty guerrillas were killed and two hundred government personnel were presumed dead or captured by the FARC.[11] It was a huge hit for the government's army.

Juaquin was assigned to empty out the guts from the corpses before the heat bloated them. Next, he helped to stuff them in body bags, and to load them onto another chopper. The bodies of the government soldiers were to be returned to the cities and to their families, and the bodies of the guerrillas were to be accounted for back in Bogotá. Juaquin worked silently in blistering, stifling heat.

He lifted corpse after corpse. At first, he was attentive to handle the body bags with respect, and when he absentmindedly dumped one and it bounced off the dirt, he silently reprimanded himself.

With his sleeve, Juaquin wiped the sweat off his face and sensed the blood splattered on his forehead and at the corners of his mouth. He tasted salt and mud. As his adrenalin settled, his back ached. He became aware that he was starving. In his pack, he had a ration of Tex Mex, spicy beans and nachos, his favorite. The Americans had donated the meals. But he grew ashamed to be thinking about food, as if the corpses could read his thoughts.

A few faces of the deceased looked familiar.

He came across a government soldier whose ID said he was Usnavi. It was a name derived from a tag for the US Navy. Usnavi had a dime-sized hole from one side of his throat to the other where the bullet pierced. Usnavi carried in his wallet a photo of himself and his wife on their wedding day.

Juaquin could not get the image of Usnavi out of his mind. He told me, "Señorita, after this day, I thought of never marrying. If I were to stay in the army, I would be thinking of my wife draped in black." A deep transformation had taken place in Juaquin in just forty-eight hours. I wondered if before his time in the army, he wasn't quiet and reserved, almost sullen. Most of all, he tended to tense up around my brother, whom he associated as the boss, as the one who made decisions and who might fire him. When he spotted Alejandro, his eyebrows quivered as if he were telling himself to stay sharp and impress him.

But in all the time that Juaquin and I spent together, there was a departure from the seemingly tense and introverted bodyguard. One day, finding ourselves blocked in a traffic jam, I turned up the volume as loud as the car stereo would go. Shakira was on the radio, and I lip-synced. Juaquin joined in, and once the song was over, I lowered the sound. Around this time, our rapport was taking the shape of the friendship I had once shared with Angel as a child.

"Listen," Juaquin said, "this is funny."

He told me that Martin Guerre, Santa Nena's donkey, was once stolen. "There was no humor in that," he said. The horses' blacksmith, a freelancer from a nearby town, reported that he'd spotted Martin Guerre tied up to a fence, on a side road not too far. The animal was easily recognizable, being so ugly that he was cute, like a gigantic—albeit angry—stuffed animal. So mere minutes before Martin Guerre was to be murdered and stuffed into sausages—"Hey, no humor there either," I said—Juaquin and the farm's caretaker busted in to rescue him. They loaded Martin Guerre into the backseat of the caretaker's car, a Renault 4.

"We drove with a donkey snorting in the backseat of a tiny car," he said.

We were both laughing and shaking our heads.

"So that's what you guys did? That is why Martin Guerre is always frightened."

With such exchanges, Juaquin opened up about his days in the army.

"Señorita, are you sure you want to hear about this?" Juaquin asked. It was his way of softening the repulsiveness of what he was about to tell.

Several hours after another battle, his captain from Miraflores waved Juaquin over.[12] Muchacho, ven, he said. He ordered Juaquin to take two men from the FARC down to the river. The men were in their early twenties. Their hands were tied behind their back. Juaquin figured the public prosecutor was stationed by the river and he would take their statements. They were likely to receive state help to rebuild their lives (as was Leonor's case). The men walked in front and Juaquin pointed the 762 at them. The captain, spitting out blades of grass, supervised from a few paces back. Juaquin expected the captain to interrogate them, perhaps rough them up a bit.

The captain spoke into his walkie-talkie. He said there were no prisoners.

The men's black rubber boots kicked the pebbles along, and they whistled, perhaps to ease the tension. If he'd had any smokes, Juaquin would have offered them one. Down by the river, the air was clearer and birds caressed the water. The pink sun painted the horizon. Juaquin took a big inhale to unload his mind.

Shoot them, the captain said. His tone was rushed, and he motivated Juaquin with promises of leave from service.[13]

At Juaquin's hesitation, the captain aimed his gun and shot the two.[14] The men's boots flew in mid-air and their bodies landed backwards into the river. Water splashed. Startled birds took flight and feathers twirled in the air.

The river's current dragged the corpses away, and Juaquin recalled the men whistling, a moment ago, a tune from an old folk song. One victim had eyes like coffee beans, the light of boyhood climbing out from them. The other had slender bony fingers, and with age, fat would have filled them out.

If you do not have a pistol with you when you need it, in cases like this, the captain said, take a wet cloth and place it in the mouth of any rifle and fire real close to the hijueputa. His voice was mellow, matter-of-fact. That way, the coroner has a hard time identifying the arm.

Muchachos, the captain said, I'll know who the snitches are. He ordered Juaquin to shoot four men before the public prosecutor arrived.

Muchacho, that's how it's done, the captain said, no regret in his voice.

The captain justified murdering former FARC because, he told Juaquin, otherwise the justice system would keep them—the "chusme," the "vermin," he said—alive and living off the taxes of honest Colombians while in some foundation or non-government entity. I became afraid that in telling me this story, what Juaquin wanted to communicate was that Leonor was in danger. She was recuperating in NGOs and she survived from government subsidies that came directly from our taxes. Had he told the captain about Leonor's history and her whereabouts?

A few days after the captain shot the men, he called Juaquin into his office. He told him the paramilitaries were looking for soldiers like him—disciplined—and he asked if he was interested. The paramilitaries were known as the military's freelancers. "Paracos" invaded locales where the FARC had strength and support, and assassinated FARC members, left-wing activists, unionists, community leaders, or anyone whose rhetoric had communist or socialist tints.

Juaquin was speechless.

It's good pay, the captain said.[15] A paramilitary's salary ranged from US$366 to $488 for three months.

Your families will be better protected this way, the captain said. Colombia will be a better place because of the paramilitaries.

The way Juaquin spoke of this day, I had to lean forward to hear him, afraid of interrupting him.

"I realized the paramilitaries were not for me," Juaquin told me.

"Good. I am glad you are not with them, Juaquin," I said. There was a tiny buzzing in my ear.

"I did feel strange when I first came to work here, to have to wear a tie," he said. "I had to borrow one from my brother." Juaquin's brother was once my mother's bodyguard, and my mother and he got on well. When he left us because his new-born prompted him to realize he could no longer be human armor, he gave Mami a tiny silver vase that fits one rose.

My nephew and I had been baking a cake in my grandmother's kitchen when Juaquin knocked and asked if he could come in and we could chat.

Juaquin recalled that the captain carried in his chest pocket a tattered photograph of his three daughters, ages twelve, eight and three. The two youngest wore pink bows in their hair.

"The captain was an assassin," Juaquin said to me. "I am *not* afraid of the captain," and I understood that Leonor was safe, that I was safe. As a journalist, paramilitaries considered me a snitch.

Juaquin and I moved to the kitchen table and drank sodas. My nephew mounted his tricycle and pedaled around us. One of the wheels squeaked. Next, the kid climbed on to Juaquin's lap and drank a mini-size yogurt drink.

Juaquin was purging himself of the images, of the guilt. I understood that his telling me had taken much negotiation on his part. His hesitation to speak came from the fact that sum-mary execution of any captured combatant or civilian is a grave violation of international law.[16] Juaquin knew that I knew this. What was he expecting from me?

At the kitchen table, his hands quivered. His face appeared ashen. He was tormented, and to see him that way frightened me.

"You will write about this?" he asked, as if begging.

Still I had nothing to say. Was I meant to relieve his remorse? In silence, I offered him my company. We drank sodas. Baking supplies lay on the table, and now, with the cake in the oven, the cleaning up remained.

Juaquin said the army rewarded soldiers with one day's leave for every dead FARC. After the incident with the captain, he and Jorge were given three weeks of vacation. During this time, he awoke at night, haunted by visions of legs with rubber boots, soaring in mid-air. Blood diluting in the river. Everywhere he went, he felt eyes judging and heads nodding disapprovingly at his shaved army head. So he stayed indoors with the curtains closed.

"It's what happens in the army," I said as if in a way of absolution.

He gave a forced smile.

From the ages of eighteen to twenty-three, Juaquin had been a car mechanic. He was fired because he didn't have proof he'd served in the military. For six months he was unemployed. He grew bored of taking handouts from his older brother, so he joined the military. He didn't like to consider who he became while in the military.

CHAPTER ELEVEN

Not long after Consuelo's murder, Leonor languished on a bench on Mocoa's main square, and an older señora asked, politely, her wrinkled face glowing with kindness, if she could sit next to her. Leonor would never forget the moment—it was an unusually windy August day in 1997, and as the church clock struck four o'clock, it seemed to be saying, "get on with your day." The old woman had heard about the hardships in Leonor's family as chatter continued throughout town about what God-forsaken trouble *esa niña* found dead with pins in her eye might have been up to.

That afternoon, the señora offered Leonor a job in her produce stand in the main outdoor market.[1] The señora had a maternal manner though she'd never had children of her own, and from the start, she called Leonor "Corazón." The time spent with the old lady turned on a switch in Leonor's life, and she flourished under the old lady's guidance and friendship. Leonor moved in with her at the end of the month.[2] She earned her room and food by helping to sell carrots and yucca and onions. The routine of the market—its opening before dawn, laying out the produce to entice passersby, and the paycheck, too—gave Leonor pride. She interacted with customers and built social skills. It opened up her network within Mocoa.

What Leonor witnessed at the market was Mocoa's undertow, a dark funnel not visible to the untrained eye. Sealed boxes were moved around now and then, and merchants knew that they might contain arms, ammunition and the supplies of war (as well as processed cocaine) and a contact from the FARC moved them. Simultaneously, community leaders arranged to smuggle refugee families out of town, away from threats. At nightfall, children and women lay down in truck beds, tucked under burlap sacks, and at daybreak, they descended to the streets of Bogotá, Bucaramanga or Medellín.

Weeks after moving in with the old lady, Leonor got an additional job as a waitress in a nightclub. "El Patrón" had a usual table—set in a corner, and teeming with a display of pork, steak, potatoes, lentils, and rice—where he ate and drank with associates. Beautiful women sat with the men, or stood behind them. Though Leonor kept her distance, she studied these women, the way they dressed and put themselves together. With a few pesos left over from her jobs, Leonor had bought clothes. Some outfits were tight, and her breasts had sprouted, though her waist was still a girl's. She was thirteen years old.

At the nightclub, Leonor noted that the women's smiles were meant to set the men at ease, to please them. Their movements were timed to blend into the men's conversations. They shimmied their breasts in rhythm to the music blasting from speakers, and Leonor was stunned the first time she heard of a girl presented with the gift of a surgery to enhance her bra size.

Some nights, under the dark light of the nightclub, she spotted a man with eyes the color of onyx. A black mustache, and bulging biceps. She found him attractive, and she waited for him to show up in the evenings. She studied him from a distance. Later she would know him as Commander Tico.

A few hours before dawn, Leonor left the nightclub. Some mornings, Redhead was waiting on the curb for her, and she gave him the leftovers that the club's kitchen set out for employees. SUVs were parked in a line in front of the club, and Leonor's eyes followed the girls who departed in the cars. She knew that what went on at the club could change a girl's fortune, and she imagined the new adventures these girls might be embarking on.

After a few hours of sleep, by mid-morning, Leonor went to work for the señora in the produce stand.

One day, her brother Leo came to the market and made a point of walking past Leonor. He was with his friend, Pedro. The two wore oversized jeans strapped below the hips and baseball caps worn sideways.

Leonor called after them. Leo!

He smiled and walked back to her. Hola, Leo said. His voice was hoarser than she remembered, wisps of a dark mustache on his upper lip. He pointed—proudly—at his high-top running shoes. He said Milton had bought him the shoes. They made his feet appear oddly big.

Leo told Leonor she was slaving away for too little money. He looked her up and down, and he and Pedro paraded away. Pedro looked back and winked at her. His eyes shone like copper and his hands were large like a man's. Leonor's face flushed again. Pedro was one of a handful of boys who came to Mercedes's house looking for Leo.

Days before, Leonor had spotted Leo in the distance with boys about whom the señora said, Corazón, they are no good. The señora gave them a quick not-trusting look. Some of them stole from the market and intimidated customers. Months later, Leo confided to Leonor that Milton had forced him, as a test, to rob people at knifepoint. He had little remorse.

Christmas passed. Lent came and went. The Mocoa gossip told Mercedes that the old lady from the market wanted to adopt Leonor, and Mercedes rushed to retrieve her daughter. She was amazed at the changes in Leonor, to find she was less a girl and more a young woman. With savings from her job at the market and the nightclub, Leonor had bought a few more dresses and high-heeled sandals. Every morning, she applied make-up.

Leonor was sweeping the señora's stand, and the sight of her mother brought her to tears.

Corazón, she is your mother, the old lady said. She encouraged her to go home with Mercedes.

One afternoon not long after, Leonor was home when she heard her mother's cries. Mercedes was astounded to find a gun under a pile of vinyl records and clothes while cleaning her children's clutter. Mercedes knew it was Milton's but she did not confront him because he continued giving her money for the family, much more than before, and they could not survive without it.

Milton continued working as a drug mule. He was taking more chances and earned more money. He developed a cocaine habit, his "vicio," and Leonor learned to stay away from him on the days that his eyes were hazy.

Milton's friends gave him the gun. They rode motorcycles, and Leonor got used to the roar of their engines speeding past.

Oliverio remained in Los Azules, and Mercedes was losing control of her children.

During this time, Mercedes tried to make amends with Leonor until Leonor began asking for more new clothes. Mercedes's anger erupted.[3] The two shouted and slammed doors, and hours later, Leonor returned to sleeping on the streets, and to frequenting FARC camps to fill her stomach. She came and went from the family home, each time gauging the situation with Mercedes. She continued working at the market and the nightclub.

Leonor and Pedro sat on a boulder on the outskirts of Mocoa, in a field at the edge of the jungle, and they shared a bottle of aguardiente that she had taken from the nightclub. They drank straight from the bottle. Long ago, back in Puerto Guzman, after witnessing Milton dragging Oliverio home, Leonor had sworn she wouldn't drink. She heard what was said about Pedro, that he robbed houses on the rich side of Mocoa. That he mugged people. Sometimes Leo stayed out all night, and when asked, he said he was out with Pedro.

From her purse, Leonor pulled out a pocket mirror and reapplied lipstick. The pocket mirror gave her a sense of security to check her image every few minutes.

Leonor and Pedro lay back and stared at the stars. She pretended to relax, while her breath raced. He began to fondle her breasts.

We should have asked Leo to come to with us tonight, she said. She thought if she spoke, Pedro would think she wasn't uncomfortable. Soon, the alcohol numbed her legs and her speech slurred.

Now his tongue was in her mouth. Her sense of sound magnified, and the crickets screamed and screeched. She was sweating and Pedro stroked her damp hair. He massaged her belly, her behind, her front.

No, no. Off me, she mumbled. His tongue became a serpent in her mouth.

He wrestled her to take off her dress. She lay naked, and so did Pedro. She passed out and when she awoke, her thighs felt wet.[4]

She looked at her reflection in the pocket mirror, and noticed her black eye.

Weeks later, Leonor's grandmother came for a visit. Abuelita had been a mid-wife for more than forty years. Whereas Leonor struggled to dress in a way that showed she was more than a market vendor, her grandmother had settled into the comfort of an old, half-indigenous toothless peasant who had lived her whole life in Puerto Guzman.

At her own home, Abuelita rose with the sun, and cared for the chickens in her small plot. If the family had not been displaced from their farm, Abuelita might have equipped Leonor with basic skills inherent of her indigenous background; together, they might have chopped wood, stoked a fire, ensnared animals for food, netted fish, collected medicinal plants, tanned hide, sewed clothing, beaded ceremonial jewelry, and woven baskets from dyed string. Leonor might have spoken not only Spanish, but also the regional indigenous dialect. Leonor might have aged into her role as a guardian of Pachakuti (Mother Nature), and would have taken pride in her heritage.

Instead, Leonor was bothered that the peasant-woman judged her for sleeping until noon, and going unwashed for days. Surely Abuelita didn't use to judge her? Leonor knew it wasn't always like this, this tension between her and the old woman. Perhaps the grandmother thought the girl had seen and lived too much, out in the streets and the nightclub. Abuelita noted that there were entire weeks that Leonor did not come home, and she reminded Leonor that if she found herself in trouble, she should recite Psalm Ninety-One.

"... under his wings you will find refuge; his faithfulness will be your shield ..."

In turn, Leonor rolled her eyes the moment that the old lady turned away.

One afternoon, Abuelita peered intently at Leonor. Leonor had eaten almost an entire chicken.

Leonor, are you pregnant?[5]

No, I am a virgin, Leonor said.

That's what your mother told me at your age, Abuelita said. When a girl was pregnant a vein popped at the bottom of her throat, and Abuelita saw such a vein in Leonor's throat.

Mercedes's screaming could be heard several blocks down the street: You've gone from girl to whore, all within a few months.

She slapped her daughter across the face, but Leonor did not react.

Sergio and Luis watched and cried.

That same afternoon, Abuelita boiled water, and of sober mind, dumped in two handfuls of dried ayahuasca leaves. She always carried a supply with her. Ayahuasca is a hallucinogen. Abuelita saw ayahuasca as nature's way to put a person in touch with the subconscious. She drank two cups of Ayahuasca tea.

Leonor! she called. Leonor lay crying on her bed. Abuelita whispered a prediction: Men will be your downfall anyway. She handed Leonor a cup of the tea, her bony old-lady hands signaling to drink up. Quick, while it's still hot, she said. The tea was bitter.

Abuelita poured her granddaughter a second cup, and herself a third.

I like how ayahuasca makes me feel, Abuelita said. With a fan made from dried palm tree leaves, she swept the air around Leonor. The old lady's eyes followed contours: tiny arms, tiny legs, tiny toes, which only she could see. Vamos, vamos, she whispered, in the same manner she might cuddle a newborn.

Abuelita danced around the kitchen. Sweat dripped from her freckled forehead and her bearded chin, and she fanned herself.

Leonor giggled.

Abuelita chanted—and giving in to her grandmother's powers as a healer, enamored to discover Abuelita's gift, Leonor whispered the words of Psalm Ninety-One alongside her.

This was the first time she witnessed Abuelita high on ayahuasca. Her grandmother returned to Leonor's side and blew forcefully around her head. May you go now, with the angels and the Virgin and our Holy Lord, she whispered. Abuelita lit a cigar and made *pah, pah* noises, continuing to blow around Leonor's aura. Saliva dripped from her cigar.

Minutes later, Leonor vomited in the kitchen sink—the first signs of the miscarriage.

Abuelita's teachings remained in her heart. Leonor often repeated to herself: "If you say, 'The Lord is my refuge,' and you make the Most High your dwelling, no harm will overtake you, no disaster will come near your tent."

Leonor told me: "That boy raped me."

I listened.

"I was going to name the baby Consuelo if she was a girl."

For three days after the abortion, Leonor dozed. Every few hours, she awoke and when she remembered the business with the baby, she cried herself back to sleep. On the second day, she overheard Mercedes telling Abuelita that she'd done the right thing. The elders had taught Mercedes that ayahuasca was only for sacred ceremonies, and since Mercedes respected the elders, she never used it to bring on her abortions. But Leonor was now the same age as Mercedes when she had her first child, and life had taught Mercedes it was impossible to raise numerous children in poverty. She also understood she could not control them and force them in the rightful path. Leonor returned to wandering the streets in a trance, with each corner she turned, she regarded her family with further detached affection.

CHAPTER TWELVE

One evening on the street in Mocoa, a FARC sympathizer approached Leonor as she was getting through the darkest hours, laying low, under a streetlight on the side of a road. She told me, "The man convinced me that coming with him to a FARC camp was the better option, you understand?" She referred to prostitution.

She also meant that as a street child, by-passers plugged their noses, no pretense at hiding their disgust. Was there anything inferior to that?

On the way to the guerrilla camp, ambling on the desolate jungle paths leading away from Mocoa's periphery, the man thrust her onto the prickly ground. His violent hands tore off her dress, already tattered and soiled from drifting the streets. She was helpless, her screams annihilated by the wild, by crickets and hulking birds, and the cries of teethy monkeys and insatiable boars and tigers. All done, the man wiped himself, and proceeded ahead.

The man and the girl arrived at the FARC camp after dark. Her dress in rags, she felt naked and exposed. Sweating, daunted, forlorn, she was grateful for the presence of other people, of a meal and clean attire. She accepted FARC fatigues and black rubber boots. She was assigned an AK-47 and ordered to join exercises in arm maneuvers.

During those weeks, Leonor and the group crossed a side road, and most mornings she bumped into a young man, a civilian. He waited at the corner to greet her and flirt with her. The AK-47, the fatigues, the exercises in arm maneuvers, it all meant she had formally joined the group, and she was losing her nerve. The young man whispered to her that he would help her to run away.

Just tell me when, he said.

At first, when she turned to him for help, she was testing how far he would go, but she was also desperate. She was now obliged to participate in strenuous physical exercises. Food was scarce.

One morning, earlier than usual, Leonor sprinted ahead of the group, in hopes of finding the young man. She was panting when she spotted him.

Let's do it. I want to leave the FARC behind, she told him.

Leonor and the young man set out, hiking through mountain paths. They heard the echo of bullets blasting across the valley, and they knew that FARC were trailing them, hunting them. They picked up the pace, running further into the bush, uphill, onto a gravel road. FARC warriors were narrowing in— they could hear the men's screams and threats.

In oversized rubber boots, Leonor slipped and tripped. The young man dragged her, then he carried her. She was bleeding between her legs. In looking back, Leonor thought it might have been a miscarriage.

"'Because he loves me,' says the Lord, 'I will rescue him; I will protect him, for he acknowledges my name ...'" Leonor felt Abuelita's vigil over her, and she found strength.

They reached Mocoa's streets, and the young man turned back to hide in the wild.

Breathless, Leonor knocked on her mother's door. Mercedes was home. Sergio rushed to beckon Milton.

That evening, Milton took Leonor back to his place. Through his drug contacts, Milton had found protection from FARC. He told Leonor—now fourteen—she had to stay with him. Leo had already moved in with Milton and so Leonor agreed. Government therapists helped Leonor to understand that Mercedes and Milton had decided the children must live with him to keep them safe from FARC recruitment. At the time, Leonor assumed the reason she spent this time living with Milton was because her mother was broke, or she could not cope, or both. It was quite the opposite. Mercedes figured Milton's drug contacts might keep her children safe, and Milton agreed. Since Milton was the oldest son, he felt responsible for his mother and his siblings. He often made decisions based on what he thought was best for the family, though it had not appeared to Leonor that way at the moment.

Milton's set-up was a lifetime away from the mosquito-droned huts where Leonor and her siblings grew up. His place had an oven and a proper flushing toilet. Milton liked to show off his financial success, and on the table, he laid his money out like a fan. The next minute, he slammed his fists down on the table and the bills flew in the air. He rarely went anywhere during the day, and instead he slept in and lounged around the apartment in filthy clothes. Paranoid someone was watching him, he kept the blinds closed. Previously he could do one hundred push-ups in a row, but now his weight fluctuated depending on his cocaine use. He gorged on pizza, and Leonor dared not say his stomach was flabby. Some days, he zoomed his motorcycle across town to the putas, with whom he was a preferred customer.

In the face of Milton's unpredictable rages, Leo made Leonor feel safer. The two were a comfort to each other. A month passed, and Milton seemed to have forgotten to lock up his siblings. Leonor and Leo ventured outside. They got matching tattoos of an L-shaped vine on their thumbs.

Leonor assumed the men who often came to the apartment in the evenings were drug traffickers. Hearing them talk, Leonor detected intonations from elsewhere in the country. One afternoon, Leo told her the files the men brought contained the information on the people Milton had to kill.[1] He was now a hired killer, part of a bigger gang that moved illegal drugs. Leo said he'd known for weeks about Milton's jobs.

Do you want more ice-cream? Leo asked. He had taken money from Milton's drawer.

She shook her head, and saw Leo as a stranger.

In the next instant, she thought of sharing *her* secret, about the man—Commander Tico, her crush—who came occasionally into the nightclub where she'd once worked as a waitress. When she'd spotted him at his usual table, she finger-combed her long chestnut hair and arranged it to rest on her shoulders.[2] She pulled out the pocket mirror and inspected her face. She tied a knot on her T-shirt to expose her belly, and after setting one brown beer bottle on the center of a tray, she raised the tray above her head. Purposely, she strutted past the man and flicked her hair. She bumped into the man's chair, and she laughed. But his attention was on chasing shots of Crystal aguardiente with Aguila beer.[3] He ignored her.

The thought of him made her heart race. She looked for this man wherever she went.

But she did not tell Leo. She was distracted by the way some of Milton's friends had looked at her earlier, with that curled-lip, head-bobbing gesture most commonly reserved for healthy-looking cows. Leonor was blossoming, her hips widening, her bosom filling out.

Six months passed and one evening, Leonor returned to Milton's giggly-drunk, humming a vallenato: You cause me wounds, all in my world is solitude. She slammed the door behind her. She flung off her high heels. Her hair smelled of smoke.

I was waiting for you. Milton's voice was deep. His being there at night stunned her, and even more so, the certain fragility in his voice threw her off. In the time in which she and Leo had lived with Milton, she avoided being alone with her older brother. The one light bulb that still worked flickered, and although it was half-dark, she thought Milton was quickly zipping up his pants.

Come. Sit here with me, he patted the seat on the couch beside him. He had beer breath. Her oldest brother had never been one to wait up for her. Her mood shifted to utter sadness: Milton's eyes taking her in, absorbing her womanliness. The way his arm was half-up, the elbow resting on the back of the couch, and his chest open as if to receive her, warned her—Be careful. She started to step back.

She saw Leo's wallet and his jacket on the wooden box.

He's dead, Leonor thought, and her calmness surprised her. She looked at the L tattoo on her thumb, dizzily, recalling Leo's pubescent voice saying, "L" stands for Leonor and Leo. She stood up and hugged Leo's jacket, his scent.

Leo had spilled details of Milton's jobs to someone, and Milton's bosses sent another assassin to kill him.[4] Without Leo, Leonor no longer felt safe to stay at Milton's.

Leonor found solace in Redhead. He was a constant friend for many years. He was someone with whom she could share a laugh or watch the soccer game on a TV somewhere. She returned to life on the streets alongside Redhead.

CHAPTER THIRTEEN

One day, a FARC recruitment note was slipped to Redhead, and he was afraid not to obey its orders.[1] Leonor showed up at a FARC camp, alongside Redhead.[2] I asked her: Did she follow Redhead because he had become her boyfriend? No, she told me, how could I presume that! Redhead was not enough of a man for her, so he wasn't a boyfriend, she said. She went with him because she was out of options. If she returned to Mercedes's, her mother would dispatch her to Milton's, and she feared Milton.

As we talked about it, both of us, we picked up on two facts. First, in the power structure of the FARC, young boys exercised authority—and were encouraged to demand sex—from girls. Redhead was attracted to Leonor, and it might have been that he brought her along in hopes that the general scene in the camps would lead to him sleeping with Leonor.

Or—and this was much more likely—Redhead was looking to be rewarded, even just to be regarded favorably, for bringing another body to the FARC. Leonor found it odd that she had never before thought of it this way. In her own life, Leonor understood so well manipulating others for her own purposes, and she was understanding how others might find her useful.

Welcome, the man said, and he slammed down his AK-47 to shake Leonor's cold hand.[3] He wore camouflage, like everyone else in the camp. This was the man from the disco! This was his camp—he was Commander Tico—and he was in charge of twenty people, mostly women. The FARC emblem was displayed on everyone's sleeve—F.A.R.C. embroidered over the yellow, blue and red of the Colombian flag.

You've come to stay, Commander Tico said. It was a statement. He seemed to be speaking to and looking only at Leonor, though there were other compañeros, including Redhead, standing nearby. Leonor noticed the man had a twitch in his crow-black eyes.

When Leonor spotted him around Mocoa, her face flushed and she dropped things. It was the allure of a teen girl towards an older man. But the señora at the outdoor market became agitated, very nearly spooked, whenever he neared her stand— his towering height and his confident stride gave an allusion that he was looking for his next prey—which, of course, Leonor interpreted as dominant and so was charmed by him.

Now, at the FARC camp, the man was clean-shaven and had a buzz cut and a golden tan. He didn't remember Leonor. She smiled at him. His shirt was tight and his biceps stretched the material.

Two women signaled Leonor to follow them to a tent where they cornered her. The plastic tarp walls rustled to the beat of the wind.

Take off your underwear, one women demanded. Leonor didn't consider what this might mean, only—feeling wobbly from hunger—that in another five or ten minutes, she might eat.

Leonor took off her underwear. The two women whispered to each other but she couldn't hear what they were saying. They checked inside her pubic hair, parting strands in the middle to check the skin. The older one smelled Leonor's panties. This older one, who was indigenous, had long dark hair hanging loose below her shoulders and so straight, it was as if she'd ironed it.[4] Leonor did not remember seeing either of them on past visits to FARC camps.

The younger one slammed Leonor's legs open. You have rashes? Itches? she asked. On her engagement finger, she wore a thin rusting ring that dyed her skin purple. Leonor thought her plain. "Actually," Leonor said, "she was on the ugly side." She was the tomboy, who would challenge Leonor for Tico's affections. She took away Leonor's pocket mirror.

I'm kind of cold, Leonor said to the women in the tent.

But neither of them cared. If a girl got a sex disease, she had to pay a fine. The fine was doing extra strenuous work like gathering wood or digging latrines.[5] You may have a sex disease, you look the type, said the tomboy to Leonor, then you give it to someone who gives it to us, and we have to serve out the punishment.

Without warning, the older one injected Leonor's left arm.[6] She did it quickly but not painlessly.

Leonor was given a birth control shot, and it marked Leonor as Tico's possession, as one more girl with whom the much older commander could do as he pleased. And now Leonor was no longer free to leave.

In some ways, Leonor was lucky that she was injected with a birth control shot: Often, young girls in the FARC were given an IUD, which could cause sterilization, especially in teen-age girls.[7]

Moreover, in the FARC, abortions were considered to be a type of birth control.[8] They were carried out under butchering conditions. During the time Leonor was Commander Tico's compañera, abortion was the number one cause of hospital visits in the FARC-dominated southern part of the country.[9] In national statistics, abortion was then the second cause of death for all women in Colombia.[10] Until 2006, during the time that Leonor was in the FARC, abortion was illegal in Catholic-ruled Colombia.

Hours after the women injected Leonor with birth control, Commander Tico led her to his tent for the first time.

What's going to happen ... she asked Tico.

Hush.

He took off his pants and guided her head between his legs. Nobody said no to Tico.[11]

Though she liked him, at first, she didn't want to be with him, and she was scared. He was thirty-four years her senior. She shook her head; her heart pounded faster. She told me, "When he first forced me, I was not in love with him." He raped her, and she became his sex slave.[12] The sexual violence, over time, contributed to effacing the memories of who she was, where she had come from, what had happened before. It made it easier to become Sofia, the FARC name which Commander Tico picked for her.

Within days by Tico's side, as she became aware of the special treatment the commander gave her, Leonor embraced becoming Sofia. She was not made to gather wood, to dig latrines, to watch the fire, or to stay awake through the night to guard the camp. As Leonor changed from homeless girl to trophy girl, some of the other women were jealous.

That ghastly scar, Commander Tico asked one evening, what happened to your legs?

I got caught in an electrical fence, she said. Leonor had convinced herself that her scar resulted from when Leo dared her to jump on a horse, and it bucked her off, thrusting her into the fence. But—she knew in her heart—the scar was from when her mother beat her after she opened up to her that Oliverio had raped her.[13]

Tico laughed. What do you mean an electrical fence? He kissed her stomach.

Instead of answering, Leonor asked for what she wanted. You know, si quieres, she said, you can have someone get me some shampoo for my hair, if you want. And some lotions for my body. The town isn't far. That's if you want me to be clean. Just for you.

The next evening, Tico presented her with the shampoo as well as jeans and T-shirts. The night after that, he came into his tent, where she was waiting, and brought her the lotion. He'd sent the redhead boy into town to buy them. Soon, she was armed with confidence.[14] She did everything Tico wanted her to do; she was proud that the others envied her. It's not my fault that Tico worships me, she told them. She began to call it love.

Her squad—Leonor, fifteen other teenage girls, and four young men—had proven their loyalty to Commander Tico. In turn, Tico had stood out and gained the confidence of the FARC "Secretariat," the head-honchos. He was the fifth highest commander in the Southern Bloc, a group of about two thousand combatants. Certainly, he had power and influence; you might say he had the stature of a governor. Commander Tico's rank was why he and his group had the privilege to stay in a house—one in a hamlet by the Caquetá River in Putumayo Department—with beds, a kitchen, and plumbing.

Most evenings, he called for her, "Sofia!" He wasn't tall, but heavy-built—hostile, ready for war. When he walked, his feet thumped on the floor. His face was square-shaped like a bull's, and he had short-cropped dark hair.

He ordered her to put on lacy lingerie he had chosen for her. She was a pre-pubescent still unfamiliar with her body.

Heavy techno music blared, and it drowned out her pain. Though minimally furnished, the house had top-notch stereo equipment, and Commander Tico had several cell phones. Through his drug contacts, he acquired the latest technology, and anything else he wanted, including sexy nightgowns and G-strings for Leonor to parade around in.

Often, after behaving violently towards her, he returned the next day with more gifts for her, perfumes, tight-fitting clothing, lipsticks. Leonor learned to ask him for what she wanted. The other girls eyed the gifts with jealousy, and Leonor behaved as if Tico did not hurt her. She had a camera, and she wore her new clothes to pose for photos.

She was the youngest girl in the group, and for Tico, it was a status symbol to sleep with her. She was considered the purest. Tico also had relations with other girls and women in the group, rotating them as he pleased.

Other evenings, Leonor and the women in her FARC squad spent the hours stuffing stacks of bills into small plastic bags, and then using duct tape to seal those in larger plastic bags. The money came from drug trafficking. It was a subject that we had spent years circumventing, and for Leonor to bring it up—to willingly disclose her participation in drug trafficking meant I had made progress gaining her trust. When I mentioned her group, the 41st Front of the FARC's Southern Bloc, to military experts, their eyebrows raised. ("It surprises me, you—from a respectable family—would know this despicable woman.") Leonor's front was known for its entanglement in most stages of drug trafficking.[15] It oversaw the cultivation of coca leaves and its harvesting, as well as the leaves' transformation into cocaine powder, and its distribution domestically and internationally. Commander Tico was involved in all these aspects.

In another room in the house, the group had stored boxes of fatigues, non-perishable foods, arms, and ammunition. Commander Tico was also in charge of arranging supplies delivery to other squads and columns. With the money obtained from drugs, and as the FARC formed contacts with other international narco-based groups, they acquired illicit arms and built a powerful arsenal.[16]

While the women worked sealing the money in the sacs, the men lounged around, watching TV, and drinking, and getting high. Music—techno, salsa, vallenatos—as well as the cocaine powder, helped to keep them awake through the night. Their energy shifted from dancing on top of chairs, the table, and the kitchen countertop, to feeling lethargic and depressed, and falling into impromptu naps of only a few minutes at a time.

More than once, Leonor took in the bills covering the entire dining room table. For her, the sight seemed a dream. At least six garbage bags, filled to the brim with Colombian pesos, were on the floor. Those nights, Leonor often thought that a bag of money would have changed life for her family. She wanted to know how she could get some of it to Mercedes, but she also knew that was impossible. To betray Tico meant death, even if he favored her.

While in the house by the river, did she understand what was happening? Was she aware that to remain alive meant not trusting anyone? When other girls went in the bedroom with Commander Tico, did she understand that in a heartbeat, the others in her group would inculpate her for anything? The tomboy—the latest girl to pique Commander Tico's interest—was taking every chance possible to displace Leonor.

Yet, it seemed that Leonor also understood that to be under Tico's command was less dangerous than withstanding conditions in the bush. Lowlier foot soldiers took shelter in tents, cooked over campfires, and defecated in trenches. Every day, they faced the threat of deadly parasitic diseases; and most days, a Blackhawk helicopter, carrying the government's elite soldiers, traced their whereabouts. Such threats, which then seemed on the borders of her life, would soon move front and centre. It seemed that this time she was much too involved to attempt running away, mainly because the commander maintained his eyes on her.

At dawn, Commander Tico strapped the bags of cash to his motorcycle. He went alone to bury the money in the ground. He made several trips, and then he reported to the next commander up in rank, who was assigned to dig up and transport the money. Only the two of them knew the exact location.

Over half of the FARC's funding came from drug cultivation and trafficking. The United Nations Development Program calculated the FARC annually earned about US$204 million from drugs, while the Colombian Attorney General's office calculated the FARC annually earned as much as US$1.1 billion.[17] It was hard to know, for certain, how much money the FARC made from illegal drugs, and any number was an estimate. The FARC earned about another US$500 million per year from kidnappings and extortions. By 2000, during the time Leonor was in their ranks, they were considered the best-funded insurgency in the world.[18]

During this time, Leonor reconciled herself to living beside Commander Tico, and as far as she could understand, she did not have a choice. Where else could she go? Who could she turn to for help? She believed that her mother did not want her home. Sometimes late at night she imagined her twin brothers playing on the street. She wasn't able to think about them without coming close to tears.

The months of rain came, followed by the dry season that scorched the countryside. One afternoon, Leonor mounted a motorcycle behind Commander Tico. As they rode on and gained distance from the house by the river, the butt of Tico's machine gun poked her stomach, and bundles of cash in his pockets rubbed against her.[19] She closed her eyes.

After half an hour, Tico turned off the motor at the entrance to a rustic campesino hut that reminded Leonor of one of her childhood homes. A weed-thin man came out.

Comandante Tico, como esta? The old man addressed the commander as "patrón" and "su merced." He tipped his straw hat, a symbol of respect.

Tico asked if he had readied the sacks of coca leaves. Then, he informed the old man the day and time when someone would come and pick them up.

The old man nodded—si, patrón—and stared at the ground. The old man reminded Leonor of her father, of toothless and wrinkled Oliverio, the same submission in his face and body language. As the two talked, Leonor checked her reflection on a compact mirror. Tico ordered her back onto his motorcycle.

Middle-ranked commanders like Tico fomented gunpoint authority over campesino farmers, mostly after 1982, when, following the FARC's seventh conference, they resolved to violently "tax" coca in FARC-controlled areas. It was known as "gramaje" or "revolutionary tax." This included a tax on the growers of the crop, at about US$50 per kilo of coca base; a tax on the local buyers, up to US$200 on a kilo of coca base; a tax on production in laboratories in their areas of control, up to US$100 for every kilo of cocaine produced; and a tax on airstrips and flights that departed from their territory, another US$100 per kilo, according to InsightCrime.Org.[20]

Leonor dug her knees into the motorcycle saddle. She thought that Tico's smell, of the cologne he applied, was classy. The wind washed over her face. If she regarded Tico as an authority figure, as a rich sought-after boyfriend, she could ignore his abuse. She wrapped her arms tighter around his waist, closed her eyes, and let the world worship her.

But the world that Leonor chose to see—the boyfriend with stacks of cash, the sexy clothes, the techno music blasting from stereo speakers when in the house by the river, and all the drugs she could want—was fragile and frightening. A moment dancing developed into screams and fights.

One night in the house by the river, her eyes were squeezed shut to numb her heartbreak, and when she opened them, Tico was crying. It was very unlike him to express emotions, and Leonor was petrified.

The commander rose from the bed to snort strips of cocaine. His eyes were red stars, the rising veins of his neck bursting through the skin. He stumbled to the bathroom. He dropped a plastic bag of cocaine on the floor, and Leonor took a pinch of the powder. She held it up to her nose and snorted it. Under her breath, she was counting, impatient for it to take effect. The nearly two years that she had spent by Commander Tico's side, withstanding his verbal and sexual abuse, was taking its toll.

Tico returned, settling next to her on the floor. He pulled the sheets off the bed and wiped his tears with them. In her brother, Milton, Leonor had seen similar mood swings, also triggered by drugs.

But now Leonor, too, was high, and nothing mattered. She looked at her reflection on a mirror, and she was stunned to see her mother looking back at her—the sadness in the eyes. The image of Abuelita, the grandmother who had once seemed an island of calmness, came to Leonor, and she recited Psalm Ninety-One.

Leonor turned her attention to the window and stared at the ripples of water on the river. The reflection of the sun on the water was blinding. She plotted to drown herself. It was a matter of understanding how near to death she was coming. Many times, her group came close to being shot to death by the government's army. Once, she played roulette with a loaded gun. Another time, she drank poison. It seemed Leonor needed the experience of dying to know she wanted to live.

One evening, Leonor walked out of the house by the river. She arrived at Mercedes's doorstep by nightfall, the pale light of the moon came through the overcast sky. Mercedes knew there was little time—the FARC had their eyes on the family. Days prior, FARC recruiters looking to surge their numbers in the mountain camps had barged in and lurked in the bedrooms for the twins, Sergio and Luis.

In the months prior, Mercedes had become a community organizer. She formed a neighborhood watch of mothers determined to not tolerate one more child snatched away by the guerrilla.

With the help from the neighborhood mothers, Mercedes got word to Milton that Leonor had returned home. Milton rushed over to the family's house on his motorbike. He picked up his sister and took her back to his place where the men with the guns convened.[21] He locked her inside his apartment, and warned her to stay away from the windows and to keep the curtains drawn. Milton did not leave her sight, and Leonor had assumed it was due to his cocaine use but—in therapy Mercedes clarified it was not so—Milton was doing what he could to save her from being taken back to the FARC. He felt guilty for Leo's murder.

By the next morning, as Mercedes had predicted, half the town was on the prowl for Leonor. She had information about the house by the river, about the quantity of rifles and ammunition and supplies stored in the house, about the drug trafficking and the influx of money. Leonor was to be found, to answer for running away and for betrayal. Tico's men roamed the streets. A glimpse out the window, and you could see the guerrillas' black rubber boots. You could hear their whispers and smell their smokes.

For close to a month, Leonor obeyed Milton and she stayed locked-up, in hiding in his apartment. She was under the protection of Milton's associates, other drug traffickers. Leonor ate regular meals and slept. Some of her anxiety lifted. But she was still a teen-ager yearning to break free from her brother's control.

One evening, when the roar of Milton's motorbike confirmed he was out of sight, Leonor stepped outside his building. The FARC had not stopped looking for her. Within the next hour, she was back by Tico's side. This time, Tico's group was stationed in a camp in the bush.

Leonor expected a FARC trial for running away, but what angered her the most was the tomboy's behavior around Tico: the girl's glowing eyes, the smiles the two produced in one another, his hand reaching for hers. At sunset, Leonor had spotted the commander taking her into his tent, and by evening, neither had come out yet. The tears came to Leonor in a torrent, dribbling onto her fatigues, reddening her eyes. What most upset Leonor was her special treatment as the commander's trophy girl had ceased, as if during the weeks she'd been away, he forgot about her. He'd spent only a handful of nights with her. Leonor wanted to gain back Tico's attention.

The night guards were sleeping, and above, the pregnant moon urged, Leonor, go![22] And so Leonor ran, barefoot, the twigs and pebbles gouging the soles of her feet. She did not know where she was heading and she tripped on the root of a tree. She gathered herself up and ran on, the sound of the rushing waterfall calling to her to throw herself off the cliff. But quite suddenly, she lost her nerve, and she sat on a rock.

She heard the sentinels talking. She gathered herself up and continued to run.

But two guards caught up to her. They gripped her by the elbows and dragged her back to Tico. They shoved her toward the commander and she fell in the dirt.

With her girly voice, she addressed her lover, I am cold. She adjusted herself, enough to flash a naked breast—but only for his eyes.

Commander Tico shook his head. Leonor had run away again, and though she did it with the intention to win back his affection, she had embarrassed him.

The sentinels tied her up to a tree, her arms pulled behind her back.[23] Shortly after, the tomboy appeared from nowhere. Sofia, you are a whore, she said to Leonor. She'd been waiting for the chance to say this, and she kicked mud that splattered on Leonor's face. Her spit landed on Leonor's shoulders. She threw Leonor's compact mirror in the mud. She stamped on it and walked away.

Later, the tomboy returned. She slapped the barrel of an AK-47 from one hand to the other, not far from Leonor's face. Sofia, the tomboy said, there are poisonous snakes here.

Throughout the night, Leonor sobbed. As dawn broke through the jungle canopy, she tasted the dew. Her mouth was pasty, her ankles swollen. Ants feasted on her knees, elbows and ankles. Red welts formed all over her body. The string that tied her up around her wrists had begun to cut through her flesh.

The next morning, Leonor was locked in a barbed wire cage alongside policemen and government soldiers—FARC prisoners of war kidnapped during attacks to government military bases. The cage was out in the open, exposed to the elements. Toucans whistled. Crickets chirped. Other animals answered in snickers and snorts.

The denseness of the jungle blocked out the sun. Her clothing, the FARC fatigues, torn to scraps, buttons missing, remained damp and moldy, and her skin moist and itchy. Every three or four days, the prisoners were led to the river, to bathe. The men stared at her and masturbated.

She smeared mud on her face to dissuade their intentions, to hide her good looks, her womanly aspects, though with her clothes in shreds, she was essentially naked.

Vengan, marranos, aquí está la comida, said a former compañero.

At one corner of the cage, there were buckets filled with mashed up beans, rice, and raw corn, and a crust of mildew grew on the food. Rainwater overspilled the buckets. Some days, the food smelled of gasoline, and Leonor knew not to eat it. At the other corner, there were plastic buckets assigned as toilets.

Anyways, in the end, we will kill you, said another former compañero.

Leonor estimated she was held in the cage for nearly three months. She grew pale and emaciated. She broke into fevers. She crouched on the ground holding her stomach, in agony from lingering cramps, and she bled, perhaps from yet another miscarriage. The flesh around her wrists was still tender from when she'd been tied up.

The other men, who were also penned up, stared at her, dismay apparent in their faces. She heard them whispering about her, in a manner that said they had determined that she was already laid out for burial.

She felt very lonely. She begged God to take her.

She told me, "The pain in my soul was that my mother never wanted me, that I had no one to watch or care for me, that I was completely alone and I never had anyone I could count on. And to know that I was going to die and decompose in the jungle."

Another day, she said, "In the cage, I made jokes and everyone laughed. I danced and people clapped."

I considered this to be another of her attempts to avoid my commiseration. It was in her character to reject pity.

During the time imprisoned in the barbed wire cage, Leonor awoke to Tico untying her. He had to be quick, before the compañeros came back from washing up in the river.

Are you going to kill me now? she asked him.

Hush—he placed his finger over her mouth—and he carried her back to his tent. Her head limped, her one arm dragging behind her like a broken wing. Her hair an insect's nest.

Agua. Un poco de agua, she said.

He laid her down on his cot and he spread a blanket over her. Sofia, please, do not run away again. Promise me that, he said.

She was confused: many times he'd forced himself on top of her. But, she rationalized, he picked *me* out of all the girls, and that meant *something*.

If you run away, Sofia, I can do nothing for you, he continued. From a brown paper bag, Tico pulled out bits of a stale roscon and he fed her.

I want to go home, she whispered. The thought of her mother's rage sunk her deeper. She imagined she took the AK-47 and shot Tico. I'm that strong. I'm fearless, she told herself. She imagined she saw Tico's blood, deep red, almost black, forming a puddle behind his head, and Leo was holding her hand. She felt warm inside Leo's embrace.

Leonor opened her eyes. The world was spinning. She imagined Tico saying, I have been wanting to tell you, I want us to be a couple again. Instead, he was ordering her to apologize publicly. Then I can give a big speech and forgive you, he said. I'll punish you with physical labor and no more. Por favor, Sofia.

From under his cot, he pulled out a bottle of orange soda, a Colombiana, and he held it to her lips. She gulped the soda, fast enough for the fizz to spurt from her nose and she choked. He laughed.

It can all go back to how we were, Tico said. She stopped crying. She wanted to believe that, after all, there was some good left in the commander. This time she did not fight him when he forced himself on her.

Minutes after, Tico led Leonor back to the barbed wire cage.

Some weeks later, the "war council" started in the early morning.[24] Leonor faced a FARC trial for attempting to run away. FARC law dictated death was the punishment for desertion.[25]

The two young men who captured her—the sentinels— were the accusers. The rest of the group, all twenty warriors, was the jury.[26] Center-stage, Leonor sat on the ground, hugging her knees, shivering. Clay covered her face, her hair, her raggy fatigues. She shivered.

Tico cleared his throat, summoning his authoritative voice. He began, Sofia has been convicted of escaping. Of treason. But her life will be spared. He took a breath and concluded the trial before it had started.

There was anger from the men, envy from the girls, and from all, loathing for the prisoner.

Sofia was a traitor.

Who knew for sure that she wan't a snitch for the enemy?

Sleepiness washed over Leonor, and again she heard Abuelita's lullabying.

Tico spoke above the group's shouts, sentencing Leonor to one hundred trips of carrying wood, five hundred meters of excavating trenches for battle, and one hundred meters of digging latrines.[27] And a one-page essay explaining why she ran away.

Sofia should be made to cut her hair, the tomboy demanded. Or at least she should go elsewhere to serve out her sentence.

Agreed, Tico said.

Leonor was dispensed fresh fatigues, and was dispatched to an area of the country that was unfamiliar to her.

CHAPTER FOURTEEN

In "La Nevera" or "The Refrigerator," a camp set in the mountain peaks, frigid, and elevated enough for snow to stick, Leonor was conscious that she might not survive. She was sleepy and feverish, and her feet and hands were numb from the cold. In that camp, any water left in containers overnight turned to ice. Heavy winds blew out the fire, and it rained steadily. Her fatigues, as well as her socks and boots, remained wet, often frozen stiff. She longed for the comforts of the house by the river. She maintained that saving her from death meant Tico still had feelings for her. She carried photos of herself and Tico, and throughout the day, she glimpsed at them. If someone asked, she described his gifts to her.

From what another woman—a FARC nurse—said, Leonor inferred worms were growing inside her skin. Leonor had symptoms of leishmaniasis, a parasitic jungle disease. Welts had formed around her wrists where she'd been tied up weeks before, and the area was now swollen into hives. The FARC nurse said the hives were causing Leonor's fever, and the FARC nurse kept Leonor on doses of aspirin. Leonor survived mostly on crumbs of brown sugar, panela, and she was hungry most of the time.[1]

At night in "The Refrigerator," Leonor confided her worries to Mother Moon. She tallied time by tracing the moon's growth from a sliver to round again. Leonor's body, too, passed through phases, swelling and cramping. She hoped she might be pregnant. Tico had surely forgotten about her. In the FARC, a girl had to be controlling and manipulative to stay at the top of the pack, and Leonor pondered—how would Tico react if he knew she was carrying his baby? If the tomboy had not been around, would things have been different? Surely, there would have been another girl.

Leonor felt tortured by the sight of the compañeros around her, for many of them had voted to kill her at the conclusion of "the war council." She was sure they would shoot her if she let down her guard.

Before she had set off for the mountains, Redhead—who was perhaps the only friend she had—took her aside and counseled her. She had to change her attitude, maintain her calm, be in control of her feelings, if she wished to stay alive.

The mountains of "The Refrigerator" were entirely FARC-controlled. Every day, adolescent combatants from throughout Caquetá department, from Fronts Thirteen, Fourteen, and Fifteen, arrived in the camp. All together, there were about forty-five minors.

One day, the teens were divided by new squadrons and assigned to columns to prepare for combat. Each practiced maneuvering an AK-47, and following commands to slither on the mud floor like a worm and to squat and lunge like a cheetah.[2] Some of the teens erupted in spontaneous giggles as adult commanders counted off drills. To the teens, it was a game, and they did not register the danger ahead. Leonor told me, "Yes, yes, truly, the psychological work the guerrilla does to a child is very motherfucking—muy hijuemadre. It is brainwashing, completely."

In the valley below, hardly visible through the bush, the town of Doncello looked like specks of dull tinsel. Most of Doncello's residents were FARC sympathizers, and many had relatives in the FARC. The majority made their living from the drug trafficking supply chain. In the mornings, Leonor took in the sun looking out over the town, and a bright band that lit the bush—in strokes of yellowish brown and emerald green, darkened by periods of rain, frost, and intense heat— and it was not possible to make out where the bush began or ended.

Not far from Doncello was the Larandia Military Base. On a map, the military base seemed a small dot, the State holding on to its last remnant in this vast rural territory—but it housed elite counter-guerrilla soldiers, and their Blackhawks and Hercules, and their high-tech communication and intelligence-gathering systems.

At five a.m. one day, FARC commanders ordered Leonor and the other teens to descend the mountains, down the slush and muddy banks, and attack the military base. The commanders directed the teens to kill, and to kidnap police and army personnel, and to destroy Doncello's infrastructure—the bridges, the scarcely supplied health clinic, and the only schoolhouse. Doncello was barely a town, more like a settlement of zinc-roofed, dirt-floored shacks, and Leonor and her compañeros threw explosives and blew them up. They fired at civilians, at mothers and their children.

"We were all children," Leonor said. "Kids, kids"—as if she wondered what it might mean to be a child. "We caused great damage."

At Larandia Military Base, the government's special force soldiers kept the engines running on the Blackhawks and the Hercules planes. Their incessant drawl was the alarm that warned a teen Leonor to keep moving through the bush. "Those days were like living inside an action movie," she said. Her fellow soldiers fired up at the choppers. They cheered and told each other they were courageous. The army retaliated, tracers blazing down from the Blackhawks. Leonor lay still in the weeds. She didn't have the energy to move.

Los marranos disparando sus marranas, a boy said.

He was repeating what the adults in the FARC often said: "The pigs firing their pigs." The FARC's name for an army's helicopter was "pig." As Blackhawks approached, their wash flattened the trees and left Leonor exposed. She scurried to avoid becoming a target—but lost her bearings. Her heart clenched.

The "marranos" continued firing down, and she knew to keep moving away from the action, adrenaline pumping through her. She developed a chronic cramp in her leg. It was the leg with the scar, where once Mercedes had beat her with electrical cords.

Along the way, she found others who had survived. They huddled together, and stayed on the move for days. The FARC camps were too far away to retreat, or they had been bombarded by government helicopters. Leonor remembered what had happened with Tico and the tomboy, and she was angry, wanting to use her Ak-47 not against the "marranos" but against the FARC.

Maybe the ninth or tenth day on the run, she stumbled upon teens' shredded bodies. Bloody. Bloating and putrid. The gunshots and grenade explosions continued. The rockets shook the ground every few minutes. The drone of the Blackhawks oscillated between faint and ear-splitting. In the evening, in the darkness, motionless silhouettes stood in the paths—bush or boulder or corpse?—the entire valley aroused fright. Under the moonlight, boulders took on the appearance of white skulls.

Leonor continued to be unwell, the fever lingering, beating her down. One morning amidst the chaos, the FARC nurse pulled her by the hand. They walked through fields, Leonor focusing on putting one foot in front of the other. Her pack was too much to carry, and she put it down. At the end of a dirt path, there was a farm house. They knocked on the door. The farmer and his wife were not in a position to refuse rifle-pointing FARC members.

In the center of the room, away from the windows, there were two mattresses piled up, and from under them, two sets of little feet stuck out. They were the farmer's children. Next to them, the farmer and his wife sat and prayed, and offered the children words of reassurance. Outside, the sounds of war continued.

Frantic and finding herself out of options, the nurse plundered civilian clothes from the farmer's wife. The nurse changed out of her fatigues, and forced Leonor to do so as well.

Sometime later that afternoon, the explosions stopped. From behind the window, Leonor took in the trees in sight reduced to fragments. Government soldiers could be spotted gathering the dead—which could only mean one thing, the FARC had retreated.

Una puta guerrillera, she heard a soldier say. He was standing a few feet away from the farm house, in the shadow of a giant tree, and he was searching through Leonor's pack. In her rush to take cover inside the house, she had forgotten about her pack, and the soldier had stumbled upon it.

Government soldiers burst through the door. They separated each person, including the farmer, his wife, and the two children, who were by now in hysterics. There was no denying

Leonor and the nurse were both guerrilleras: their face and hands were sunburnt and chapped from time spent outdoors. Their feet were swollen and blistered from trekking. Their hands, too, were calloused from lugging equipment and chopping logs for the fire. Around Leonor's head, marked on her forehead and on her hair, was the outline of the tight cap she had worn hours prior. Further, the nurse was heavy-set, thick-lipped, and her intonations were from the Coast, very unlikely that she would be a farmer in this region, or even a relation to the farmers.

Leonor said, "The soldiers would have picked up right away that I was a guerrillera. From my bad mood. From the way I responded to them. From my mindset. I was dead already."

The soldiers interrogated Leonor and the nurse. Their stories did not match. They couldn't keep denying their connection to the FARC.

I can give you information, Leonor said.

What do you know? a soldier asked.

Outside, within her view, the soldier who was combing through her pack, found a pair of her G-strings, pink-laced and ruffled, a gift from Tico, from months ago. With a stick, he waved the lingerie in the air.

A whore here, he shouted. Una puta.

Inside her pack, the soldier also found the photos of Leonor in fatigues, posing and smiling, and hugging Tico. There were images of parties held in the house by the river.

I am a commander's girlfriend. I know stuff, Leonor said.

Every girl like you is a commander's whore, said the soldier.

Four other soldiers slapped her face, one at a time, as if the men had decided beforehand that they would take turns. Blood spewed from her nose. A boot kicked her in the stomach and the ribs. Heeled over on the ground, she choked on her blood. Two soldiers lifted her by the arms.

I will tell you who I am, she shouted. My mother is a pistol. My father is a Galil rifle. My brothers are gunshots. I am part of Front 41 of the FARC's Southern Bloc.

I will fuck that puta guerrilla, fuck her up the ass.

We should strangle the puta.

Right here, hang her from this tree.

Puta guerrillera es una perra.

Two soldiers aimed their revolvers, and nudged her, pushed her, forced her to walk in a line in front of them. With her back to them, she heard their taunting.

Now. Shoot her.

Throw the grenade at her, hija de puta guerrillera.

The soldiers tied her up, and threw her in an army truck, and brought her back to Larandia Military Base.

They shoved plates heaped with corn and potatoes in front of her. She was famished, not having tasted a bite in days.

You hungry? a soldier asked.

Another poured gasoline over the food, and force-fed her.

They laughed. They intended to inflict more suffering, of course. Here was a girl—a kid—alone and vulnerable whom they could use like a punching bag.

Word spread that she was a commander's girlfriend. The photos circulated around the base. Another soldier asked her if it might have been easier to be a paid whore, and the comment became a running joke among the men. We captured a puta, they said to one another.

Later that evening, a government nurse cleaned her up. She gave Leonor antibiotics to lower the fever and topical cream for the welts on her skin. Leonor was suspicious of the woman's kindness. She guarded her words (as Tico had instructed her). She had spurts of weeping, and uncontrollable shaking, and fury.

The government nurse asked how old she was.

I think I am seventeen, Leonor said.

It's all going to be okay, added a soldier nearby. His words were not to appease Leonor, but rather meant for the public defender—who at that moment walked into the room, carrying a clipboard—to overhear.

The public defender asked if she wanted to call her mother. The thought of speaking to Mercedes turned Leonor's rancor towards her mother. Conflicts between them would take years to be resolved.

The next day—her file recorded the date as April 23, 2001, the day she arrived at her first government home where the social workers, Don Enrique and Doña Susana, welcomed her—a quick test determined Leonor was, in fact, pregnant. Leonor said the baby was Tico's. (Doña Susana said, "It's not clear whose baby it was.") Leonor was not far along and she soon miscarried.[3]

CHAPTER FIFTEEN

Less than two months later, in June 2001, I first met Leonor at Don Enrique and Doña Susana's. From outside, the first halfway home looked like other houses in the neighborhood, Victorian style with white metal guards on the windows. Until 1985, the neighborhood was the most fashionable and elegant in Bogotá, and four former presidents had resided in the area. Then, the neighborhood became middle-class, characterized by the Carulla supermarket and the park nearby.

During my initial visit, I hesitated to ring the doorbell. I looked back at Juaquin, who was parked across the street. He nodded, Go on. A social worker opened the door. She was curt. I had lobbied my case to a government minister, and the social worker did not like receiving a phone call from a government minister's assistant instructing her to grant me access to the teens. She excused herself, and I was left alone.

I joined a group of teens watching TV. Their bodies said they were adolescents though their fidgeting and their elusive-ness, and their initial coldness and suspicion of me, spoke of war. The image on the screen was blurred with static but we could make out the voice of a politician making anti-corruption statements. I joked about the irony of politicians denouncing corruption, but no one laughed and I felt silly. My heart was palpitating; my hands trembled and I hid them in my pockets.

"What are you all watching?" I tried again that day.

"The news," said Homero. "Some prisoners escaped from a prison last night."

Taking that interaction as a welcome, I sat with them. Homero was the first former combatant I befriended. His hair was cut into short rows of porcupine-like quills, and his whole head was dyed sky blue. Social workers encouraged the teens to do their hair any way they wanted because that was promoting their individuality as opposed to the FARC where it was all about the collective.[1]

Homero was the home's established leader. I sensed this when the woman who worked in the home's kitchen asked him to come into the dining room, so that he could lead the rest of the group toward their meal.

Leonor, too, thought getting close to Homero would serve her well. One Sunday morning, I walked in on her and Homero making out. She was rubbing his neck, his hand was up her thigh. They stopped when they saw me.

Around this time, Homero asked Don Enrique if he could have sex with a girl (an unspecified girl) in the home, as per FARC custom of asking the commander for permission. Don Enrique said he could not prevent him from doing so, and I wondered if Homero had Leonor in mind.

There were several other halfway homes in the neighborhood though their exact address remained a mystery. The halfway homes were sometimes targets of bombs or attack.[2] Conditioned by war, Homero put in place an evacuation plan.[3]

"It's essential," he said, and showed me a detailed mock-up that included head counts and the locations of doors and windows. The tree outside one window had a branch for crawling out on, so as to drop onto the front lawn and bolt away. The inner stairway led to the roof, from where you could launch yourself onto the roof of the house next door. Homero was adamant the evacuation route was what mattered most, and not the therapy nor the remedial lessons in phonetics and arithmetic, which took place once a week in a computer lab. Though most of the teens had never seen a computer before, they learned quickly how to surf the web for porn.

One morning, when we were together after several days during which I had not seen Homero, he seemed distant, and I pointed at an arts-and-crafts project displayed on a table and asked him: "So, a camp is always like this? Do the guards always sleep on the outside? On the four corners like these plastic figure men?" He nodded, his eyes bulging, and I thought, Bingo, war talk always excites Homero. He kept nodding at me, as if to say, Of course. Where else would the guards be? Playing naive, I learned, was a good way to make Homero feel important.

Another day, I was alone, balled up in a chair in the hallway between the kitchen and TV room. I was distracted: What was behind Leonor asking if I knew the whereabouts of the FARC nurse captured alongside her? "She told the army she was underage. She isn't. Can you find out where she was taken?" Leonor asked me. No, I would not get involved.

I was exhausted from coming to the group home every day. I craved going home and getting in the bathtub to read—for pleasure—under the bubbles.

Along came a boy I had noticed before. His body was slim. Skimpy. He had fluff on his upper lip, not the sturdy hairs of a grown man. He walked turtle-slow, on crutches, and he had a huge scab on his left leg, from the bottom of his knee to his ankle. I smiled at him, then looked down to check something in my notes. My contact lenses were drying up, and I squinted. I was scanning my notepad but noticed the boy's long fingernails. How strange, I thought, that his nails are long and still clean.

My mind wandered again. Where could I get sushi take-out in Bogotá?

Homero yelled, "Don't." His voice was rigid. "Stop." It was an order.

I looked up. The boy with the long fingernails had his crutch raised in midair and was about to hit me over the head with it.

"Stop. Okay?" Homero was stern.

The boy looked at Homero, put his crutch down, and scampered away. Homero and I cemented our bond then and there. He was willing to protect me. I smiled at him yet tried not to make a big deal of what had just happened. I wasn't ready to digest that I could have been hurt.

I felt secure because it had been confirmed that I was under his protection. Our relationship transformed, from my thinking of him as a kid to his assuming I was the one who needed to be sheltered.

Another dynamic was at play: Homero exercised his authority over his peers, and I was simply an instrument. Leonor's approval of me came from her deciding that if Homero thought I was okay, then, I must be alright.

The boy who attempted to hit me over the head had thin metal wires protruding from the toes of his left foot. A victim of land mines,[4] Don Enrique told me. According to the government, there was one victim every eight hours, giving Colombia the world's highest number of land mine victims.[5] Until 2001 the Colombian government also used land mines to protect its bases and hydroelectric power stations. The government estimated there were one hundred thousand undetected land mines in rural zones. The mines have a lifespan of fifty years.[6]

The wires held the boy's toes together, and he could walk with the help of crutches, but he would never be able to move freely again. One Sunday, as we sat outside in the sun at a nearby park, the land mine boy sat in a wheelchair. He watched his friends playing basketball. His eyes followed the moves on the court, and he screamed with glee when his friends scored. He clapped and warned—"¡Cuidado! Behind you. Good move." The scab on his shin was shrinking.

Fifteen years later, I told Leonor what had happened with the land mine boy that afternoon.

"At that moment, I became Homero's little child, like a toddler he had to look after," I said. "I was very scared coming into that house to see you."

"You mean, you didn't know how people were going to treat you?" Leonor said.

"Yes."

"You weren't the only one, many times when someone was aggressive towards us, we planned—and here I include myself—to kill that person. If we felt someone betrayed us, or used us in any way, we felt there was no other option than to kill that person. We detained Don Enrique in a room one afternoon."

They wanted to show him the teens held power over him.

"The plan was to kill him. I don't remember what he did. Whatever small issue, we thought the solution was death. That is what the guerrilla taught us, that the answer to anything was murder."

Leonor explained that the land mine boy attacked me because I showed my fear.

"If you show it, you are done for. Pan comido, Paula," she said.

For Leonor, too, the new home and the new compañeros inspired distrust. Bogotá itself, with paved roads and traffic and tall buildings, was a culture shock. Social workers and psychologists pushed her to recall events, which ended with her crying. She turned into La Llorona, weeping for her lost childhood. Doña Susana—fleshy, middle-aged, upbeat—made sure Leonor ate enough, and gave her multivitamins.

At the end of 2002, Leonor was moved to her second government home, in Girón in Santander department, and social workers cajoled her into participating in karate lessons, and swim lessons in the pool in the courtyard. Each government home was located in a certain setting conforming to a step in the former combatants' recovery, and in Girón, there was a summer camp atmosphere.

Leonor said, "It was a chance to experience the kind of childhood we had missed." She was eighteen years old.

Girón's population numbered around 115,000. From a bird's view, Girón appeared staged for a Christmas nativity. Founded in colonial times, the town's architecture consisted of two-story adjacent houses uniformed with white paint, and terraces that spread out across entire facades. When the baker opened the oven, the aroma summoned you to buy dinner rolls, and—

between her sobbing that resulted after therapy each day—Leonor marveled at the locals' easygoing life.

She walked around Girón, oftentimes limping from the pain in her leg. Therapists were forcing her to assimilate the calamities lived in "The Refrigerator" and during the Battle of Doncello and with dark thoughts bubbling, she could not reconcile Girón's quaint setting—narrow cobblestoned streets originally designed for horse-drawn carriages. The bell tower of the grand cathedral, evocative of Spain's colonial rule, beckoned to confession and Communion. In front of the church was the central square, and beyond was the park where locals sat on benches and passed afternoons playing impromptu chess, gossiping, and flirting. Doors were left unlocked because neighbors were trustworthy. Even the weather was ideal, veering between seventy and eighty degrees Fahrenheit.

Leonor returned from the walks, and the compañeros in the home were at free-play in the pool, or playing a board game. One afternoon, Leonor sat with a social worker, and in whispers, they put words on paper to the sentiments that Leonor carried around about her childhood.

It was government child-rights policy that while living under the care of the demobilization program, social workers guided the former combatants to write and produce plays about their experiences. Emotions were choreographed into dances. Every three months or so, in a theater in Bogotá's National Park, the teens from different group homes throughout the country convened to share their work, to feel less alone.

One afternoon during Halloween season, in 2004, Leonor built up the courage to recite on stage a poem she'd written. The lights dimmed. The spotlight settled on her. Her hand was sweaty on the microphone. From the audience, she resembled a boy, her long hair in a pony tail and tucked under a green cap. She wore fatigues.

At first, hesitation constrained her voice:

"They call him street child with such repugnance. He is a child of the shantytown.

He likes to spends his days in the river, looking for fish. But the fish died long ago.

The afternoon comes, hunger grips his throat. He goes to the garbage dump to look for food.

His mother washes the town's clothes. He did not have a father even for a short time.

He continues to grow. One day, they make him a prisoner.

They found him begging for food. He leaves his mother, his hut, and his town.

Rifle on shoulder, he will become a rebel, dreaming of a better world."

The lights brightened the stage. She took off the boyish cap and tousled her hair. Folkloric vallenato music blasted, and she danced with a wooden rifle. Dip-glide-stride. At the end, sweaty, as she caught her breath, she took in the audience that filled the theater. They were clapping for her, and she beamed. She embraced the wooden rifle.

Leonor returned to Girón and in the pace and lifestyle of the small town, Leonor learned to unwind, and to trust enough so as to build friendships, and to feel safe, perhaps for the first time in her life. There were nights she slept through until morning.

Some evenings after dinner, she joined a group on a stroll to eat obleas (waffles with dulce de leche) or roscones (white bread filled with guava), and to drink hot chocolate, the beverage for which the town was known. They sat under the moonlight and reveled in idle chitchat. Oftentimes, the town's troubadour set up on a corner nearby, and endowed a festive tone. Weeks into experiencing the ways of Girón, Leonor felt she could fall in love with life again.

"It was a wonderful time that I will never forget," she said.

Sometime in 2004, therapists deemed Leonor rejuvenated enough to move her to her third government home, and this time, she was sent to Floridablanca, also in Santander department. Floridablanca, with a population numbering around 270,000, was a flourishing town, with rising apartment buildings, paved streets with names, slight traffic at rush hour, and public transportation. A number of locals commuted to Bucaramanga, a regional capital, located less than thirty minutes away by car. The weather was a tad cooler than in Girón, between sixty-five and seventy-five degrees Fahrenheit.

Leonor enrolled in a local school alongside ordinary adolescents who lived with their families. Until then, Leonor had only studied in a computer lab near Don Enrique's government home in Bogotá, where she went through the motions of basic second and third grade schoolwork. Now, she was twenty years old, and she was aware that these lessons might be a last chance to receive an education. She blossomed.

But in the group home, a handful of young men—former low-level commanders—bullied the studious kids. When these young men were in the FARC, it was likely they had been obliged to sit still for hours in the stifling heat, as older commanders lectured them about the FARC's roots in the Communist party. The boys had not been taught to read, and they were embarrassed about their illiteracy.

Because of the bullying, Leonor hid the joy schoolwork brought her. She retreated to the room she shared with three other women to study and read. She found school assignments were less complicated than the ongoing therapy, and she rose early to go over lessons. She felt pride when teachers praised her.[7] In the home, Ricardo became her friend. Though he was not as enthused about schoolwork, he encouraged her to continue her courses.

She dedicated herself to addition and subtraction, followed by basic multiplication and division, some reading and writing. In less than a year, she passed remedial fourth, fifth and sixth grade.

The school principal admired her persistence. When the school put on a small fashion show, Leonor was selected to participate as one of five models. On the day of the show, other women applied make-up on Leonor. They cut and styled her hair, and they helped her to put on and take off the dresses she modeled.

Before Leonor was due on the catwalk, she examined herself in the mirror. Since therapists began helping her to flesh out memories of her family, the bond Leonor had shared with Consuelo was taking a deeper meaning. What would her dead sister say if she could see Leonor as a model in a fashion show? It seemed not so long ago that she watched Consuelo standing in front of the mirror admiring her newly dyed platinum-blonde hair.

On the catwalk, Leonor blushed. There was a thunder of applauses from the audience—"They were admiring *me!*" she recalled. Up until then, Leonor assumed everyone saw her for whom she had been, the hungry child in rags. Up until then, she had held on to the false idea that her own mother could not stand the sight of her, and so it must mean that her place was, indeed, in the wretched streets.

At the end of the show, after taking a bow, she studied the audience, a small crowd of students and parents from the school and a few of her friends from the home. Her eyes fell on Ricardo. A therapist had asked her to keep a list of things to live for, and she had added Ricardo to the list.

Every day, Leonor attended group therapy with the compañeros, the fifteen women and twenty-five men in the home in Floridablanca. They met in a solarium where ferns flourished, scaling walls and wrapping their stems around one another.

Therapists encouraged the group to openly listen to each other's experiences, and to accept the other's feelings. It was a plea meant to counteract the bullying. As weeks turned to months, the motto in the halfway home became: Here lives love and not war.

As a group, they finished each other's sentences. They consoled one another, and they alerted the social workers if a compañero's spirits were sinking. They shared clothes. They took turns cleaning the house, cooking and washing dishes in the kitchen, and watering the ferns in the solarium. ("I know what you will say, and yes, it was a hippie commune," she said.) Leonor learned to receive and to reciprocate kindness and empathy, and it felt like coming upon spring after a long winter. She also was given the space to behave like a teen-ager, though she was years past adolescence.

While in group therapy, while sitting in a circle on the floor or squeezed side by side on a couch, the friends held hands. Leonor arranged to sit next to Ricardo.

One Sunday night, the group convened in the solarium. It was after midnight, and they spoke in lowered voices. They did not turn on the lights, afraid to summon the supervisors.

A young man adopted the tone used by a social worker. He said, Hold your compañeros with love.

Better yet, make love with your friends, another young man said.

Wild laughter detonated.

Ricardo pulled Leonor towards him, and she was aware of the narrowing space between them. They kissed. She told me, "It is what they say, fireworks, you know?" She giggled.

In the dark, enveloped by ferns, other couples paired off. Couches were moved to the sidelines, and clothes were stripped off. Collectively, they lay on the cold wooden floor—fat bodies, skinny bodies, black-skinned and pale. There were white scars and red scabs from war. But there was no teasing, no disdain at all, which surprised Leonor, to this day. Civility. The atmosphere of the home had changed but Leonor had not noticed. She had been consumed with her schoolwork, and fighting tears conjured by therapy.

Love is better than war, someone said.

Through the skylight, the stars, organized neatly on the sky, lit a path as if to another life. With Ricardo, in the solarium with the compañeros around them, was the first time that Leonor consented to sex, and the way she told it, a temporary euphoria surged within her.

Weeks later, Leonor overheard that Ricardo was cheating on her with other girls in the solarium. The sex had an effect deeper than psychoanalysis, and she was overwhelmed with recollections of her past—above all, of Oliverio, her father, raping her. Each time she thought of what he had done, it was his excuse about the blanket she remembered most. "He maintains he was tucking me in with a blanket," she told me.

She stayed in bed in a deluge of tears. Her eyes smoldered into the cracked walls. She skipped school. The spaghetti brought up to her dried up. The soup gelled and the milk soured. Flies circled an open bottle of soda. Her room smelled of stale food, of feet and sweat. Her hair grew tangled. The two pairs of jeans she owned grew big for her shrinking body.

To crack her depression, therapists moved her to the city of Bucaramanga, with a population of half a million. It was 2005, and she had abided by the State's program for former combatants for four years. She was twenty-one years old, and it was no longer required that she stay under the constant monitoring of social workers. She settled in a youth home with a dormitory-like structure, and she was granted more freedom. Ricardo was part of the group who lived with her. Each received about 350 dollars per month of State subsidies. The government only required that they continue showing up for therapy, so they remained under the rule of the government's demobilization program.

Ricardo recognized Leonor was having a difficult time adjusting, and he made it his job to suppress the sobs and gulps that came to Leonor on her morbid days. He kept her busy. They dusted, mopped, and disinfected the toilet. They learned to use washing machines to do the laundry.

With money and shelter secured, their life evolved into a game. They shopped for groceries, admiring the sauces and condiment aisle, and becoming awestruck by the choices—hot dogs, corn dogs or beefier bangers, and jasmine rice, brown rice or sushi rice. Leonor set the table for meals, and she took pride in laying napkins under the cutlery, the way that social workers had instructed. When the roll of toilet paper ran out, she rushed to replace it. In the evenings, she and Ricardo curled up on the sofa to watch TV, as if it were part of their decades-old routine. Therapists told them to avoid all news shows.

Leonor recovered her appetite. Some nights, she again slept through until morning. She credited her calmness to Ricardo. His companionship meant so much. *Thank you for the human interaction. I am grateful that you won't give up on me. Thank you for showing me that I want to live.*

Every morning, she expected Ricardo to have left her. In fact, she didn't venture anywhere without him. The more time they spent together, the more they planned the recipes to cook and jointly washed up after dinner, the more they settled into behaving as if they were already husband and wife. All Leonor really wanted, and had wanted for a long time, was to feel part of a family and to feel that she had a home, and alongside Ricardo, she felt this sense of stability. Psychologists and social workers recognized this behavior as a normal mourning for a lost sense of family and childhood.[8] However, any codependency was frowned upon in the government's program.

All this time that Leonor and Ricardo were building intimacy, social workers had been biding their time, finding out if there were empty beds in other homes, and waiting to find the right time to separate them. The following month, Leonor was dispatched to another youth home in the city of Cali, and Ricardo to Chia, a suburb in northern Bogotá. Leonor couldn't adjust to life without him, missing the businesslike way he put structure to their days.

In Cali, the quietude of nighttime and the glare of the stars and the moon that streamed through the bedroom window taunted Leonor. Others in the group home were preoccupied with their own torment and they let her carry on.

It was often dawn before she fell asleep.

At dusk one day, unable to stand the idea of another solitary night, she walked to the bus station. She could not control nightmares or painful memories, but she felt compelled to prolong playing house with Ricardo. She resolved to find him in Bogotá. She snuck onto the overnight bus, and hid in the bathroom until they were outside Cali.

The bus drove on roads safeguarded by government soldiers—in some cases younger than Leonor—equipped with machine guns, bulletproof vests and helmets. At army check points, soldiers used flashlights to peer into the trunks of buses and cars. Soldiers examined the faces of passengers for scars from shrapnel, and sun-blistered noses and chapped lips, the traits of a guerrilla. The soldiers aimed to prevent guerrillas from entering Bogotá.

The bus pulled into the main station in Bogotá in the early morning. She did not have Ricardo's address nor telephone number, and she did not have a plan. She did not have money. The cold humidity swooping in from La Sabana and the mountains that enclose Bogotá seeped through her light clothing. She felt the chill in her bones. She sat on a bench, crossing her arms over her chest for warmth, and closed her eyes. By mid-morning, the honking cars, the revving engines of motorcycles, and the intensity of the Andean sun roused her. She asked strangers, one after another, for directions to a government office. She would not give up.

She slept on a park bench that evening, and the next. This time, she was less afraid as when she'd first slept on the streets of Mocoa as a child. Her intent to find Ricardo numbed her. She forgot that she had not had a bite in days.

On the third afternoon, she found an office of the Ministry of Family Welfare. She explained herself. Social workers called the government home in Cali and confirmed her story. She was fed and provided with a shower and clean clothing.

Ricardo was summoned. Half-laughing, Leonor buried her face in his familiar chest. His smell summoned tears of joy. During one of the many evenings they had spent together in front of the TV, curled up under a blanket, she had fallen into a deep sleep and in the morning, she awoke reassured that he was still there. She yearned for that same kind of comfort. With him by her side, she could make it, she told whoever listened.

That girl has been through so much, was what she imagined therapists said about her. Leonor forced herself to smile, to answer their questions politely. Si, señora, she said to make it seem that she was not to be pitied, to make it seem that she was living an ordinary life. Si, señora, she said, no matter what was asked of her.

Leonor and Ricardo remained together in the same home in Chia, in northern Bogotá, though they slept in separate rooms. As they had done in Bucaramanga, they walked the streets of Bogotá, enthralled by cars driving in lanes and obeying traffic lights, skinny buildings that seemed to neighbor the sky, and malls blasting Christmas music. They stared in awe at the festive red and green lights. From a promotional cart at the market, they tasted chicken seasoned in curry and saffron, but they did not like it and spat it out.

Social workers in a parody of consternation—"as if they really cared," was how Leonor put it—remarked how lucky she had been to find her way around after arriving at the bustling bus station. Leonor nodded in agreement with them—Si, señora, she said—though she did not then understand what was lucky about her life.

Leonor again slept through the night. But during this honeymoon time, she was also wary of what she knew was to come. After two weeks, Leonor was sent to another government home, this time in Normandia neighborhood in western Bogotá. As long as she continued to live in government housing and cash the stipend, she was obliged to follow the rules of the government's demobilization program. To see Ricardo in Chia, she rode on two or three public buses, for two hours, sometimes longer, withstanding jam-packed vehicles as hot as ovens, traffic, sirens, horns, and loudspeakers. They saw each other less and less. Metropolitan Bogotá was after all so very vast.

CHAPTER SIXTEEN

Many residents of Leonor's new neighborhood, Normandia, had immigrated from the countryside, and most were now hustling to make it in Bogotá. They worked as bricklayers, electricians, messengers, and domestic servants. From there, the social gamut ran down to prostitutes, drug runners, and small time drug dealers. Strips of the neighborhood were rough. It was not unusual for Leonor to hear of robberies or break-ins. A few times, she witnessed feisty brawls, which rattled her. After the months she had spent in the tranquility of Girón and Floridablanca, it took her some time to get used to walking around while appraising any danger from strangers who—as happens in the commotion of city life—encroached on her personal space.

An urban landscape also meant Normandia's modest houses were built compressed to one another like crooked teeth fighting for territory. Entire streets were steadily under construction. As paychecks came in, as relatives arrived to try their luck in the city, residents added rooms, decks or another level to their homes. Streets were obstructed due to drilling and cement mixers, and amplifying the cacophony was much hammering and—because everybody knew that Normandia was a shortcut to avoid the busier main highway—the honking of jam-packed cars. The lane barriers of the thoroughfares had long ago turned yellow and patchy from strewn cigarette butts and plastic bottles and bags. In the far reaches of the neighborhood, surrounding Leonor's halfway home—her sixth one—the district was overdue in paving roads and laying down the aqueduct.

In this new setting, social workers were guiding Leonor to start taking responsibility for her own upkeep. They reminded her it was up to her—and not Ricardo—to build a life for herself.

Her days were filled by a jewelry-making course offered free to former combatants by the International Organization for Migration (IOM). In a workshop in downtown Bogotá, she sat slumped over under bright lights and strung beads into necklaces. She was focused on the task since morning. She did not wish to stop.

Within months, she expected to be placed as an apprentice to a jeweler. The other compañeros in the home had chosen training in carpentry, mechanics, gardening, agriculture, and baking.

Thick necklaces intended to hang past the bosom, chokers like collars, and gaudy knobby bracelets, all of it enthralled her. The twinkle of the beads as they caught the light. The sharpness of the stones when she closed her palm over them. The first time that she was instructed to insert feathers into the pattern, she presumed it was a joke until she saw that the contrast lit up the colors. She treasured the two necklaces that the supervisor said she could take home. Once, Tico had given her thin gold bands, but never this kind of jewelry with—as Leonor came to see it—a fashionable cosmopolitan flair.

Her eyes ached by early afternoon, by the time to return to the group home, but she was content. She took the window seat of the mini-bus that transported her back to Normandia neighborhood. Privately-operated mini-buses were the only rides to and from Bogotá to the peripheral neighborhoods. Hours were wasted idling in traffic.

The mini-bus took Leonor through downtown. She stared at the shops, cafés, and restaurants—at the people sitting outside enjoying lunch in courtyards, under the shade of tall buildings. But before reaching the arteries leading to the suburbs, the scenery changed to mechanic shops and tree nurseries. Occasionally in the distance, there was a glimpse of plastic tarps, the greenhouses where roses and carnations grew in time for Valentine's Day, to bloom inside shipping boxes en route to New York and Miami. From then on, as they drove further southwest, the sidewalks and roads were cracked, the streetlights were broken, and there emerged a trail of front-yard dumps and battered-looking houses.

Once back in Normandia, she observed the old ladies who towed carts to busy intersections, and sold homemade arepas, buñuelos (donuts), and one cigarette for one peso. It was the scene of a mother or grandmother struggling, and it made her think of Mercedes. Leonor had taken to calling Mercedes, and during their weekly telephone call, mother and daughter were rekindling their relationship. Leonor followed the social workers' cues, careful to word her feelings so her mother was not hurt, and stopping herself from bringing up episodes—at least not yet—that were upsetting to either of them. Leonor understood this was her only way forward. A priority in therapy was to rebuild connections with the family.[1]

There was so much about Mercedes and Mocoa that Leonor wanted to ask. Did her mother live in the same house, and did her twin brothers, Sergio and Luis, live with her? Did her mother still rely on Milton for money? All the therapy had made Leonor start envisioning life in her mother's home, and what it might be like if she were to return to Mocoa. Unexpectedly, there were days that Leonor was homesick for her family.

What was Leonor going through that she sought to reconnect with her kin? Her most recent therapist had suggested that she try on a religion, and Leonor remembered her mother frequenting church every Sunday, and sitting in the front pew. Mercedes had been in her mid-twenties—almost as old as Leonor was now—and Leonor remembered that month after month, her mother lit a white candle. Might religion bring a feeling of closure, of forgiveness and new beginnings?

On her walk to board the mini-bus that took her to the jewelry course, there was a storefront converted into a small Evangelical Church. Since twice a day Leonor passed the church, she dropped in one evening with another woman from the group home.

An attendant at the front greeted them. Do you both chew gum? she asked.

Leonor was amused. Gum! Go on, she said.

The woman said, Because if you two go from one guy to another, it is like you both chew the same gum and pass it back and forth to each other.

What did gum-chewing have to do with religion? What did gum-chewing have to do with dating? Though the woman was young, Leonor thought she wore the prudish clothes of a sixty- or seventy-year-old. She seemed the type to scorn lipsticks and stylish hairdos.

Even so, Leonor was intrigued, and she joined in for Bible study in the evenings. She entered the church and when the door shut behind her, the noise of the neighborhood remained locked out. Here was a much-needed respite. After two or three evenings, the faces were familiar, and that, too, was comforting. She followed along the scriptures. In the crinkling pages of the Bible, she felt she might find answers. How much responsibility should she feel for what she witnessed—drug trafficking, extrajudicial killings, kidnappings—as she stood by Commander Tico as his compañera? How much should she blame herself—and she did blame herself at times, enough that guilt kept her up at night—because, after all, she had been a minor.

The early 2000s in Colombia. How much these questions, this kind of remorse and grief, seemed to belong to those years, just as Leonor's age and personality—her attention-getting ways, a normal passage during puberty—were part of her experience. In her story, her versions of the battle of Doncello and the war council and the near-death days in the cage, was not separate from hormones, intense emotions, and mood swings. She aged, and as if by magic, she continued to believe that love, as in the soap-opera-kind, existed.

One evening in Normandia, the church receptionist's brother—Andres—introduced himself as one of the pastors. He was tall, white-skinned and blue-eyed. I'd seen photos of Andres on Leonor's Facebook page, and when she said he was kind, I agreed with her—his eyes spoke of his conviction.

Leonor continued frequenting the church, now with a frenzy to see Andres. One day, she realized it had been weeks since she saw Ricardo, her beau from the solarium, and she was getting by without him. Andres had taken over her attention.

He expected her to come to the church in the evenings after the jewelry course, and he waited for her. After Bible study, he invited her to the movies and for ice-cream, and he gave her flowers.

Andres's family and the congregation took note of their courtship, and they studied Leonor. They disapproved that she dressed in T-shirts, jeans and flip-flops, the only clothing she could afford. Their Evangelical uniform consisted of pressed long-sleeved shirts, long skirts and pleated trousers. Leonor discerned that strangers in the neighborhood—members of the congregation who had heard that she was Andres's new girlfriend—judged her attire, and thereby her social standing. It was cruelty, and Leonor allowed herself to be defined again by her appearance. When their eyes settled on her, she regressed to believing that her place was in the garbage dump foraging for nourishment.

Churchgoers documented Leonor coming and going from the government halfway home. They figured out she was a "reinsertada," a former FARC, and they were scandalized.

An ex-FARC was not who they would have chosen to be with Andres. They believed his life was replete with altruism, but not that he should take a demobilized as his wife. His family and the church community refrained from speaking to Leonor. Yet, she did her best to smile and be pleasant around them.

Andres's family and some members of the church spoke to him about breaking it off with Leonor. Their words had the opposite effect, and instead he spent more time with her. There was a tone of triumph in her voice, as she told me that she gained control over Andres, winning him over.

Leonor and Andres strolled through Normandia neighborhood, hands clasped, and she relished hearing others' gasps. She kissed him for all to see. He took her shopping, and spent his money on buying her dresses and stilettos. He liked to see her dressed up, and she liked to see the faces of the congregation when she paraded the new outfits.

Then, one day, Andres disappeared. Leonor searched for him inside the church and she waited for him outside, sitting on the cool of the concrete steps. She trembled and pushed scenarios out of her head: He had not been hit by a bus. He had not been gunned down or kidnapped. She lingered on street corners, stores, cafés, hoping he might suddenly appear. Everywhere there was a reminder of him.

Limping again from stress, Leonor hobbled around Normandia neighborhood with a somber expression. On the street, people pointed at her. Some didn't bother whispering.

She's the guerrillera, one said.

She's not a Christian, another said.

She blinded Andres.

She used witchcraft to trap him. It's good he is gone.

Through the whispers, and the fragments that people were willing to fill in, she figured out that Andres had moved to the city of Pereira. He was working in another church, and living with his extended family. He had not said goodbye. He had not explained himself to her. She felt he betrayed her. She blamed him for not standing up to the church and his family.

Then she began to think that what was said about her was right—she was worthless. She was a cast-aside, a no-good. She had been a street child, a destitute. She was party to FARC murders. She knew of the existence of mass graves. Andres was a pastor. The congregation was right—Andres deserved a better woman. She blamed herself for FARC's actions. A hole formed inside her.

She could no longer apply herself to beading necklaces, or sorting beads, or tying clasps. She showed up only periodically to check her name off the list, and so receive the government stipend.

She spent the allowance on whiskey. At first, the golden liquid burnt her throat, but it numbed and buried her anger, and she yearned for more. All she wanted to do was drink and forget. She lay on street corners and blacked out. Once, she awoke and found Andres's sister staring at her. Dios mio, Dios mio, she seemed to be saying. Leonor assumed she was cursing at her, so she spat on her.

Alcohol, drugs, nightmares, all behavior that former FARC members and former government soldiers had in common. On a weekday at seven p.m., sometime in June 2007, Leonor and a retired army major passed a whiskey bottle back and forth. They were inside the room he rented in a pension near her government home in Normandia. They had sex, often, but what passed between them had no meaning. Outside of the hostel, if they happened to cross paths on the street, they pretended not to know one another.

Andres's sister had first lured Leonor into the church by all that talk of how gum-chewing was like dating. What nonsense, she thought. About the army major, she told me without emotion, "I don't remember his name. And I doubt he knew my name." Maybe the army major didn't know she was once FARC. "Most likely was that he didn't care," Leonor said. She also couldn't remember how they met. Perhaps they started a conversation in a liquor store. It was what Abuelita had predicted: Men would be Leonor's downfall.

The army major liked cocaine. He shared his stash with Leonor. When she was high, nothing else mattered, and she sought that feeling when she entered the pension. She looked for ways to black out, to make herself forget she was alive.

When Leonor knocked on the army major's door, he gave her drugs and led her to bed. If he was away, she bought bazuco, cheap cocaine-paste cigarettes, which were easily available in the neighborhood.

Leonor finished the jewelry-making course. But her interest in necklaces and bracelets had dimmed. Instead, she accepted work as a courier delivering mail and packages throughout Bogotá. She was earning money for the first time in a job that was part of a private business community quota for rehabilitating guerrillas.

Through the years, as Leonor recounted her life, I saw that substance abuse was a bigger obstacle than she admitted. After Andres abandoned her, she stayed in therapy but descended into a black crevasse. She was part of the first generation of former combatants to pass through the government program to help them lead conventional lives, and I rooted for her success. She had the resources to build a productive life, and I took her potential wellbeing to mean that if former combatants had the will to move away from armed groups and live within the law, Colombia had a chance for peace.

But Leonor cautioned that the government approached the process of demobilization as though it could take place en masse. She believed each former combatant had her own path and challenges to overcome.

Leonor spent the afternoon with the army major in his room in the pension, and she was drunk and high as she made her way to a party in the common room of the government home. The get-together was to bid goodbye and good luck to a few compañeros who were moving on to another group home. This was not her most morose day. She was dressed up, in tight-fitting leather pants from second-hand clothing that social workers brought in. She wore red lipstick.

At the party, a bottle of aguardiente passed around. She accepted more shots.

A local reporter showed up and Leonor talked into his tape recorder. The aguardiente loosened her tongue, and she alluded to Milton, her brother, touching her inappropriately—which he had not. It seemed that in her mind she fused Milton and Oliverio's behavior. She was losing grasp of time and events.

In the common room, Leonor slurred her words and tripped over furniture. She looked down at the spinning ground, and she thought about Andres's gentle manner—and now he was gone.

The reporter moved on to someone else. A compañero was nudging her.

He was a former paramilitary who also lived in the group home. He passed the booze to her, and his stare held her. She shifted her attention to him. He wore blue jeans that slipped to his hips in the style of a rapper.

Leonor drank more. Her eyes glazed. She smiled when the young man spoke to her. In the next moment, a suffering expression dominated her face.

Sometime that night, (she later deciphered, through conversations with others) the former paramilitary guided her to a dark corner. By then, beyond dizzy, she had blacked out. The next morning, she awoke huddled under a blanket on the floor of the common room, broken bottles and cigarette butts strewn about her.

In the following days, the young man ignored her. She grew angry, and she went around wanting to hit people. She said, "Those paraquitos thought the FARC women were less than them."[2] The paramilitaries looked down on the FARC as illiterate farmers.

But Leonor blamed herself for what happened. She chastised herself as a sinner.

Soon after, Leonor stopped caring about her appearance. The alcohol and drug binges continued. So did the visits to the army major in the pension. She staggered around smelling of her own vomit. She stopped showing up for work at the courier service. Her coworkers had bets on when she would quit.

She thought about running away to look for Tico. His gifts—perfumes, toiletries, lacy lingerie, and clothes—made her the envy of all the girls. She wanted to hold on to that.

It was December 2007, and as was tradition, every corner of Bogotá had a nativity scene with an empty crib. One day, Leonor could no longer deny her growing belly. Social workers took her to a doctor who confirmed she was at least six months pregnant. In telling me, she found it comical that the social workers used phrases like, "think about your options" and "a child of God." But soon she was overwhelmed and in tears.

She was almost certain it was the paraco's child. She had not seen the army major in months. Had she? Whoever was her daughter's father didn't matter to her.

Each morning, she presented herself at the threshold of the small office where social workers stored the paperwork. The social worker on duty handed her a small plastic cup with a pill of folic acid and a multi-vitamin. She forced herself to swallow them. She was told her job now was to have a healthy pregnancy. She was allowed to sleep whenever she wanted, and to lounge watching TV at all hours of the day.

On the day someone was scheduled to speak to her about giving up her child for adoption, she felt the baby move for the first time. She thought of the child in her arms and felt joy. She vowed to raise her child. With the support from the social workers, she would try to stay away from alcohol and drugs.[3]

CHAPTER SEVENTEEN

It was early evening when the bus pulled into the depot in Mocoa. Seeing the streets where she had been homeless prompted conflicting emotions in Leonor. The last time that she was in Mocoa, seven years earlier, she was still a FARC member under Tico's command. Now she was due to give birth in two weeks' time. It was March 2008. She took in the small figure of her mother standing at the curb, a toddler resting on her hip, Mercedes's last child.

The social workers had made all the arrangements, insisting that it was a good idea for Mercedes to be by Leonor's side for the birth. Making a homecoming, Leonor wanted to let her mother know that all was forgiven, and she needed help with the coming child.

Recent phone calls between Leonor and Mercedes had brought them closer. During a call one afternoon, Mercedes had said something about coming home permanently, and Leonor told her that living in Mocoa was not in her future. Later Leonor told me, "It's a funny thing, but I can't remember now where else I thought I would end up."

On the bus, she wondered how Milton would react to her presence. Her heart raced. She felt the baby turning over inside her. How would it be with Mercedes, after all this time? Never mind. She wanted to collapse into deep slumber, as soon as she could.

Tia! the toddler called out to the pregnant woman, descending from the bus. Leonor was limping, which she always did now, when she was tired. Auntie! Mercedes did not correct him. Mercedes had felt the pain of surviving some of her children. The boy in her arms was a last chance, but then, Leonor, the one Mercedes thought would never return to her had come home.

They greeted each other, coolly, distrustfully. It would be a short visit. To continue receiving the government stipend, Leonor had to check in at the halfway home in Bogotá ten days after the birth.

Tia, her brother repeated.

I am not your aunt, Leonor snapped. Soy tu hermana.

The boy had never heard of Leonor.

In the following days, Leonor found sympathy for her new little brother.

Mercedes held Leonor's hand the moment Rosa was born in the town's hospital. Leonor was moved to see her mother smile joyfully at the sight of the newborn. Mother and daughter went home to Mercedes's, and in the days that followed Leonor was grateful for Mercedes, for her assurance of handling the baby.

Mercedes taught her to latch Rosa to her breast for feeding, as well as to bathe Rosa and put her to sleep. Leonor, too, surrendered to Mercedes's care. This had been the social workers' plan all along, to give mother and daughter a common project as a start to re-building their relationship.

As Leonor and Mercedes went about the day, they kept the television on, the daytime soap operas playing in the background. Some were set in Bogotá, and Leonor observed her mother studying the images.

Leonor began to ponder the extreme difference between Mocoa and Bogotá, and to accommodate in her mind that she had a place in both worlds. Mocoa was surrounded by jungle, and fields planted with coca plants for processing cocaine, and land mines. Landslides followed the heavy rains. Most houses were similar to her mother's, no taller than two floors. In contrast, Bogotá was a metropolis with gourmet restaurants, universities, and an opera house. Everyday when in Bogotá, Leonor walked in the shadow of towers. Not so long before, while working as a courier, she had spent time navigating the bustling streets. She learned the street names and the direction in which the traffic flowed. She figured out the bus stops as she rushed to finish her deliveries on time. Now and then, she stopped to take in Bogotá's atmosphere, the boutique's windows, the after-work crowds rushing in herds to the Transmilenio bus stations, and Carrera Septima closing on Sundays for the use of bikers and rollerbladers. Leonor ached for a chance to describe all of this to her mother. It was a matter of pride, maybe; a way of revealing all the challenges she had faced and survived alone in the big city.

Bogotá really is like that, Leonor told her mother pointing at the television.

During the commercials, she described the women who worked in offices alongside the men, and wore suits and carried briefcases. Like in the telenovelas, she said, some of these women are the top bosses, above the men.

But there were incidents she knew her mother could not assimilate. Once, after Leonor had been directed to leave a package on a desk in an office, she found the office empty. For a moment, she feigned it was hers. To Leonor's surprise, it belonged to a woman, and she was not angry to find Leonor there. Instead, having been told that Leonor was the former FARC who satisfied the government quota, the woman pressed Leonor for details about the government's rehabilitation program. ("I think she wanted to rub in my face that I was once FARC. The bitch," Leonor told me.) Her feelings were too much to explain to Mercedes. Maybe if Mercedes had visited Leonor in Bogotá, she might have understood. Social workers tried to arrange this, but the cost of the trip, plus lodging Mercedes in a hotel, was too expensive.

Days after Rosa's birth, Milton dropped by. Leonor was frightened of him until she saw him overcome by Rosa's tiny feet, tenderness in his eyes. Rosa clutched his finger and his face lit up. Leonor still expected him to hurt the baby, and when he showed up again, she always stayed nearby. One day, Sergio arrived with a bag of diapers. Sergio said they were a gift from Milton. Maybe Milton was not entirely bad-natured. Maybe he was angry because he was still grieving over Consuelo's murder. Maybe he was hard because Mercedes turned him into the father figure for all the children, laying the responsibilities on him.

With a baby, she couldn't mess up anymore. What would be expected for that baby with a mother like that. Each person passed judgment. Leonor's life choices, how best to burp the baby, who was the baby's father, all of it was discussed out in the open, already sounding like the stuff of gossip. Such was the gibberish Leonor heard from family members—distant cousins, aunts, adult nieces she met for the first time, all strangers to her—who came to the house to drink coffee.

One afternoon, Leonor had to get away. She took newborn Rosa for a stroll. Her hometown was hard to recognize. Gone were the dusty pebbled roads—where the man on the motorcycle had tried to abduct her—replaced by fresh pavement and a turmoil of traffic. At the marketplace, a multitude of vendors spilled out onto the streets, and crowds gathered around the produce. Leonor fondly recalled the señora in whose stand she once worked. ("I never saw that lady again.") What might the señora say knowing that Leonor was a mom?

Leonor shifted in her step and rearranged Rosa on her shoulder, becoming aware that she did not want a drink or to get high. She was an acrobat walking a tight-rope.

On the tenth day in Mocoa, Leonor and Rosa boarded the bus for the return to the government home in Normandia neighborhood in Bogotá. Mercedes was sad to let them go. Come back soon, she said.

One afternoon about a month later, Leonor returned from walking Rosa around Normandia to find Andres waiting for her on the steps outside the government home. Right away, he took Rosa from Leonor's arms, and she allowed him. He really did seem touched. He held the baby close to his chest, and he wiped tears from his eyes.

She's not yours so don't cry, Leonor said. Still crushed by Andres's sudden departure, it took all her might not to hit him. He ignored her tone, and hugged Leonor, Rosa sandwiched in the middle.

Andres couldn't find words to say that Rosa made him feel like a father. He had felt like a father since he first heard from church members that Leonor had been seen with a baby in her arms. Some in the congregation believed Rosa was Andres's baby, and they said to let him know was the Christian way. Or maybe they were fueling the gossip.

Limping like someone three times her age, Leonor was grateful to take a seat on the steps of the government home.

After childbirth, she had little time to rest, and the pain in her leg was worse, persistent enough that sometimes it forced her to sit down.

Andres—greatly daring—grabbed the diaper bag from her shoulder. He sat down beside Leonor, and resting Rosa on his lap, he changed her soiled diaper, and handed the baby back to Leonor.

You hold her, Leonor said. She understood what Andres was trying to do for her. Unlike before when he courted Leonor, there were no dates for movies or ice-cream, and he did not bring her flowers. For Rosa's sake, Andres concluded, they were both beyond such things.

Within weeks, he rented a house in the neighborhood, and Leonor and Rosa moved in with him. Leonor found solace in his gentle manner when he spoke to her like a pastor. It was this side of him that had made her fall in love with him. He was patient and oftentimes nurturing, and she found she could open up to him. She told him that while in the FARC, when Tico's group was in the house by the river, she'd swallowed poison before diving into the water. She intended to drown herself. At dusk, she awoke vomiting on the shore, the shadow of a fisherman standing over her—but there were no fishermen for miles around.

Andres told her the fisherman was God. God himself saved you, he said. God saved you for a reason. For Andres, Leonor was a figure of immense suffering, and it was as though she had been marked and saved from so much harm by God's protection.

Leonor signed up for a course to become a security guard. But no one—most importantly, not even Leonor herself—believed she could stay employed and afloat.

Andres's family insisted he marry Leonor if they planned to continue living together. By now, Leonor had ceased to believe in soulmates and fairy-tale kind of love. She agreed to become the pastor's wife because the pressure to feed and clothe Rosa was causing her anxiety. She didn't think through what it meant to marry, and only hoped Andres would step in and help her with the new expenses.

She was now remembering gossip from Mocoa: The baby will challenge her. Mother and baby will end up homeless. The horror, a mother like that. The baby doesn't stand a chance. The gossip burned a hole in her as she slipped on a white bridal dress. Two-month-old baby Rosa, sobbing and red-faced, was in the stroller, but Leonor didn't comfort her.

Lucky girl, a social worker said, as she fixed Leonor's veil. In Leonor's mind, the social worker meant: lucky, you are damaged goods and a decent man agreed to take you on. Lucky was also what the other women in the home said when she'd told them Andres wanted to marry her. They said she was living in La-La-Land if she thought she would be hired as a security guard. Be practical, a woman advised her.

I want to get high, Leonor thought. She programmed herself to endure her wedding day. The photos taken showed no expression on her face.

Smile, Andres's sister said, at the reception. What Leonor heard was: why are you not happy? Only God knows why my brother married you. Only God knows, and the sister crossed herself.

Andres resumed his role as a pastor in the same church. The church was to Leonor the judgment and hostility of the congregation and his family, and a roadmap for what had failed before in her relationship with her new husband. There stood the church—at the corner, where she had to walk past to get anywhere—and its red bricks and wooden doors had an expression of teasing, even taunting. It was where they were married. She avoided entering the building even on days when Andres was there from morning to late afternoon.

She began finding ways to separate her days from his family and the congregation. The people around him continued to act condescending to Leonor. She overheard his sister telling him that he had "civilized that monkey from the jungle." Once Andres himself told her that she was descended from campesinos, backward hillbillies. He belonged, after all, to the same clan as his family and his congregation. ("All evangelist shit, you get him?" she said to me.)

Leonor held back from revealing to him the little things about Mercedes, like that she did not know how to open a

savings account, file taxes, or apply for government bene-
fits. No one Leonor knew in Mocoa did any of this. Leonor
had learned these skills from social workers. After the wedding, Andres had urged her to forget her former life. He also
declared that he would never travel to Mocoa. He liked to
think his new wife would devote herself entirely to him.
Leonor understood that such was the only kind of wife he
knew, as the role models were his mother, his sister, and the
women in the congregation.

What do you find to talk about with your mother? Andres
asked Leonor one evening, after overhearing them on the phone.

Leonor took it as an affront, and believed it revealed
Andres's true nature. She could not change him.

To add to the strain between them, Leonor was breaking out
with genital warts. It caused her fevers. She felt trapped—his community defined women in terms of purity and marriageability—
and Leonor told herself that the genital warts were proof that she
was slutty.[1] She was ashamed, bleak, like a castigated animal in
pain. She endured the fevers until a social worker—in secrecy,
under the guise of government therapy business—accompanied
her to the doctor. She was prescribed antibiotics, which she hid
from Andres.

A few weeks after the wedding, Leonor began the course in
security training. She was made to run for miles, even if hob-
bling from her weak leg. She climbed fences. She developed

physical strength. After childbirth, Leonor had felt at odds that she did not fit into her two pairs of jeans, and she had a double chin. Her body was always a sense of pride, and though she was breast-feeding, she starved herself. Clumps of her hair fell out. But leaner and stronger, she was upbeat to see herself reflected in the mirror. Two or three times, men in suits and ties dropped by to observe the trainees. The sun beamed off their shiny black oxford shoes. They talked about the jobs available in DAS, the State Security Agency. They said that with additional training, some could be hired as bodyguards.

Not long after, Leonor secured a job as a private guard in a mall in northern Bogotá. She wore a uniform of blue trousers, a blue blazer and a white button-down shirt. A pistol was tucked inside a holster that hung from her belt, and the weight of it— the awareness that a weapon was within her grasp—made her feel powerful. She began to revert to feeling submissive when people called her the pastor's wife. Cooking and cleaning for Andres, she missed the respect she assumed she elicited when they saw she was armed.[2]

Of course, Andres did not tell his family nor the members of his congregation that Leonor worked as a security guard. It was his arrogance. He needed to maintain an image with his community that he was the sole breadwinner. He paid their rent, as well as their groceries, Rosa's daycare, and the diapers.

You are my wife. You shouldn't work, he said.

He also maintained that Leonor needed to look a certain way. No more flip-flops and T-shirts. That was your past, he said. He said her paycheck and the government stipend, which she received while continuing therapy, was hers to spend on clothing. For the first time in her life, she bought stilettos, several pairs. She treasured them as confirmation that she'd escalated several tax brackets. She bought more dresses, in various styles.

The women in group therapy commented on the new outfits. Que afortunada, one said. Another pinched the material of a dress between her thumb and first finger, rubbing, admiring. But being the subject of envy no longer pleased Leonor. Social workers took in her gloomy face, and they told her not to waste her chance at a domestic life. It could be a happy life.

To the world around her, it seemed Leonor had beat the odds. Look! A former FARC built herself a legal life! She appeared on course to give Rosa a stable family, which social workers pointed out when Leonor expressed negative feelings. Other women in the group home marveled: How did you do that!

One afternoon at a traffic light, while riding a bus with Rosa on her lap, Leonor observed a girl below on the street, begging for spare change. The girl walked from car to car. The girl was a version of Leonor, at that same age. The girl stopped a moment to catch her image on a side-view mirror of a parked car. Then she turned away, as if slapped by her reflection. Leonor knew that feeling.

Mercedes suspected Leonor was not fulfilled, and she was lonely, and during one of their phone calls, she said, Come home. The phone chats with Mercedes became more frequent. Leonor looked forward to her mother's voice. She liked hearing how her siblings were doing. Sergio and Luis were aware to stay away from neighborhood gangs. Sometimes Leonor spoke to her youngest brother so he could hear her voice and be reminded that she was his sister and not his aunt. Leonor began thinking of her family in Mocoa as her clan. Her eldest sister, Ligia, was married. It took several conversations for Mercedes to reveal that her husband was a policeman.

Some days, her mother mentioned Milton. Mercedes tried to persuade her to see his good side but Leonor quickly changed the topic of conversation. Then, there it was—one day on the phone, Mercedes let it slip that Milton was beating his wife. He had given her a black eye and broken bones. He cheated on her with several women.

Leonor continued to attend therapy sessions with government psychologists, and she told them she felt pride as she put on her security guard uniform every morning. On the bus to work, she was happy because she had something to do, somewhere where people showed their appreciation for her work.

One evening, Andres commented, I'm ashamed of my wife working. You need to stay home and cook my meals, and wash and iron my clothes.

Leonor suspected Andres's mother and sister were behind his words.

Seeing his words sting his wife, Andres said, Let me explain. The FARC was your past.

What did her past have to do with her new job as a security guard?

Leonor knew their marriage was unlike anyone's in his congregation. His family's pressure to leave her made his life conflicted. And Leonor's genital warts continued flaring, so she kept her distance to keep him from touching her.

You are my wife, Andres continued.

Their voices rose in argument. Rosa was alarmed and cried.

The next day, Andres announced that they would move to Pereira. A fresh start, he was thinking.

But neither of us has a job there, Leonor said.

Mercedes wanted Leonor to return to Mocoa. But Leonor knew that once in Mocoa, she would have to accept Milton as head of the family. Could she forget his violent past? Would he make trouble for her?

So Leonor followed Andres. Her hope for independence wilted.

Pereira was the center of coffee country where ruby-like coffee beans covered mountains and valleys. Palm and bamboo trees, and bougainvilleas, bromeliads and orchids, lined cobblestone roads leading to wooden portals that opened into the green yards, and estate houses with wrap-around balconies. But in the city's downtown, where Leonor and Andres settled, the fumes of cars and buses congested the air. Sidewalks were crowded with vendors peddling fruits, sweets, and deep-fried pork rinds. In a café on one of these streets, Andres and Leonor found work as servers. It was June 2008.

By now, Leonor had achieved enough schooling, vocational training, and hours in the courier service to be awarded US$7,000 for a "life project," a government grant to encourage entrepreneurship and create jobs for demobilized combatants.

A social worker suggested that Leonor partner with the café and use her grant to buy computers and relaunch as an internet café. But the computers were outdated and slow, and customers never used them.

At the end of the month, she didn't have what was due to pay her part of the café's rent.

Her new business partner threatened to call the police.

Leonor explained to him that she had spent the entire $7,000 on the computers, and so she had no income.

The business partner fumed. Once a guerrilla, always a guerrilla, he said. All you former FARC are the same, continuing to steal from honest people like me.

Andres heard the exchange. The words resonated in him. His mother and his sister also told him, whenever they had the chance, that Leonor was a criminal, a drunk, and a junkie. She spat on me once, his sister told him. Quietly, he washed down the tables and mopped the floor in the café. At the end of the day, he turned the cardboard sign in the entry window from Open to Closed.

That evening, Andres confronted Leonor. Pale and his lower jaw trembling, he asked if she had stolen the money. Be honest, he said.

No, I have not, she said.

Leonor had trusted the social worker who advised her to buy the computers at a friend's shop. Leonor called the social worker, repeatedly. She left messages, but no one ever responded. She'd been duped, she concluded. The incident planted her distrust for the government. It seemed more likely that neither Leonor nor the social worker knew enough about technology to make an informed decision when it came to buying the computers.[3]

She explained all this to Andres—no, she hadn't stolen one peso, she said to him—but his face remained blank. It was as if he was backing away from the marriage.

For weeks, Leonor lay awake at night, worry suffocating her. If she had to, she would go to jail—for whatever amount of money the café owner said she owed.

It was now the middle of the night. Leonor took in Andres next to her, his chest levitating in tranquil slumber. Her rage escalated. She could handle the guy at the café distrusting her, he was a stranger—but not her husband. Why was her husband not a source of comfort?

She hit him and screamed at him. He awoke.

Nearby, Rosa shrieked. Andres picked up five-month-old Rosa and soothed her in his arms.

Leonor moved on to the kitchen. She broke dishes. The stress of facing jail time and her disappointment in Andres prodded feelings she'd anesthetized for years.[4]

Alone in the kitchen, throwing dishes onto the tiled floor, slamming pots against the counter, thrusting glasses at the wall, her breath came quickly. Her mind returned to Tico. The commander was forcing himself inside—Sofia—in Sofia's mouth, Sofia's anus, Sofia's vagina, and Sofia bled. The commander was holding the girl down and she squirmed to get away. His hand over her mouth, his other hand not hesitating, but going powerfully to work. Invading, prodding, numbing her—and yet she fought back. She could still believe that she had the strength to stop him.

To Leonor, the kitchen and the bedroom in Pereira looked like places she had never seen before. How had she ended up here? She slipped her tongue in the hole in her mouth where Tico had punched her, hard enough that he knocked out a tooth. Barefoot, Leonor walked a circle around the shattered porcelain and glass.

In the other room, Leonor came upon a hysterical Rosa. The next moment, Leonor was choking Rosa.

Andres grabbed Leonor, threw her against a wall, and fled with Rosa in his arms.

Leonor held her arms across her stomach and rocked back and forth, and panted.

"It all happened too fast," she said. "Suddenly, the guerrilla was a mother and a pastor's wife."

Three days later, Leonor remembered Rosa. She dressed and looking haggard, red-eyed, uncombed, funky-smelling, she took the bus to the office of the government's rehab program. She would stay composed, she told herself. In an office with the door closed, she explained to another social worker that Rosa was missing.

Andres kidnapped her, Leonor said. She was concerned for Rosa, and she wanted Andres punished. He took the baby in the middle of the night, she said.

The social worker explained that Andres did not have legal rights to take Rosa. He was not Rosa's biological father. But Leonor did not want to be reminded of Rosa's conception. The government contacted the police.

The next day, Rosa was alone, playing on the floor of the social worker's office when Leonor picked her up. Andres did not put up a fight, and he didn't reveal that the little girl had been in danger with her mother. He didn't want to cause Leonor further trouble.

Andres stayed away, but on the phone, he checked in on them. With every phone conversation, Leonor opened up more to him in the easy-going manner of when they first met, when there was no pressure to be wife and husband. It was easy to pour out emotions when talking while staring at a blank wall; she disliked having to look at someone reacting to what she was saying. With him on the phone, she sorted out her feelings, filing them neatly in piles, all the ugliness of the five, or six years, that Tico did as he pleased with her. Andres told her not to blame herself. She was touched by his concern for her and Rosa. Andres could have ditched her, forgotten that he had married her. It felt good to be taken care of, even if via the phone.

I used to play roulette with a pistol, Leonor told Andres. I'd put the gun to my head but the bullet never fired.

Andres was silent. She could hear his breathing.

She said to him, Ha! The bullet never fired! Oy!

The conversations drained Leonor. She wanted to sleep. She broke into fevers, and with fevers came waves of genital warts.

I love you, Andres told Leonor in a phone conversation over Christmas 2008. Will you move in with me?

Afraid he would stop giving her attention, she agreed.

He rented an apartment on the outskirts of Bogotá, in Fontibon neighborhood.

Each day, Leonor strolled Rosa to a park nearby to get fresh air. She made lists in her head as she thought about her new life with Andres.

#1. His family lives a one-hour drive away and there are no reasons for me to see them.

She resorted to the list whenever she was anxious.

#2. Andres never hits me.

She half-heartedly continued showing up for the government therapy, but more as a way to fill her days. Since the computer saga in Pereira, she had not regained trust in anything government related. She felt she was living the same day over and over, the hours filled with the tasks of motherhood. She was restless and sought distractions.

She told Andres one evening that she wanted to work, to have a purpose.

He didn't respond. She watched Andres tearing his fork into the chicken she'd cooked for him, and she grew irritated.

She pressed him.

He piled white rice onto his fork then looked up at her.

For a long time, he said, he'd thought about his role in her life. He decided he needed to protect her from herself. He worked long hours as a server in a restaurant. In his hours off, he was working as a pastor in a local church. He could provide for the three.

But Leonor couldn't understand why he wanted to take on the role as provider for another man's child. She thought he would grow tired of the situation, and then what? She believed tragedy was to come.

Andres reminded her that the stress of working as a courier led to alcohol and drugs. He thought Leonor's anxiety about problems at the internet café led to her choking Rosa.

Leonor's face grew flushed. She felt a swelling in her chest as she anticipated what he might say next. Anger rose up her legs and through her spine.

#3. Andres gives me money. Suddenly, that point on her list no longer seemed a blessing.

That evening, Leonor put Rosa to bed. She turned out the light. She returned to Andres and he was already sleeping. She watched him. She touched his face. Again, she wanted to stab him. She once asked me, "Why would I want to hurt him?"

She sobbed. Andres turned his body toward her and scooped her in his arms.

Leonor weaned Rosa. The girl spoke her first words, and she learned to walk and run and climb. She blew out two candles on her birthday cake. In taking care of Rosa, Leonor passed the days, weeks, months. It gave her something to do. But now it took all Leonor's strength to get out of bed. It was all she could do. Every day, she fought the desire to drink and do drugs. Mother and daughter stopped going to the park. The window blinds remained closed. The air inside turned stuffy. The dirty dishes and laundry piled up, and cockroaches and mice appeared. It was April 2010.

Andres continued working in the restaurant. He was often tired from being on his feet all day.

One evening, he asked why she had not tidied up.

Leonor was insulted. He didn't want a wife, he wanted a servant. She didn't want to keep having the same argument. The searing rage and desire to break things came like a mighty storm in her. In agony, she retreated into her room. She cursed, implored the devil, made bargains, and came to tears. Her mother had told her that if she continued to live with Andres, she would snap again, she would return to alcohol and drugs.

The next day, Leonor asked the government to find her a new home.

When she left Andres, she didn't know she was pregnant with his child, Dahlia.

Three-month-old Dahlia laid stomach down over her mother's shoulder, drooling. Dahlia was born in Bogotá. She had inherited Andres's fair skin and blue eyes. Nearby, coffee-skinned Rosa, almost three years old, watched television. She sang along to the songs, her brown hair hanging in strings over her face. She smiled, all charm. It was nearing March 2011. Leonor was a single mom, and they lived in Bogotá's outskirts.

Two men arrived one afternoon, unannounced. They were dressed in dark suits, white shirts, black ties, and polished black shoes. They extended their hands for a shake and introduced themselves as envoys from DAS, the state security agency.

The chubby one smirked when he studied Leonor. She was dressed in a thin white shirt snug around her bosom.

A pyramid of dirty dishes was piled on the kitchen counter-top. Paint chipped from the walls. One of the men swept crumbs and rice off a chair before sitting down. The men glared as she limped around. The pain in her leg intensified with stress.

One of the men suggested that she needed money.

It was true. The government stipend wasn't enough. She'd searched for a job, but no employer would take a chance on a former FARC.

The men went straight to the point, proposing that she infiltrate a criminal gang. She would report on the whereabouts of a businessman who'd been kidnapped. The pay amounted to about US$150,000 dollars.

Leonor nodded. With the money, she could buy a house, a car. Buy the girls proper mattresses, nutritious food, send them to school. She could buy herself more clothes.

One of the men placed a card on the table. Señorita, I look forward to working with you, he said.

Ten years into rehabilitation, Leonor was considered a success, ready to recycle her skills for the government's benefit.[5] Considering the DAS offer, Leonor fixed herself hot agua de panela. The brown sugar tea was her dinner. She re-heated three-day-old chicken for the girls. She would accept the DAS job, even if it involved guns and criminals.

She was a missed payment away from eviction.

Across from her, Rosa looked pleased, and said, TV.

Rosa held Dahlia's hand and hummed to the baby. For Leonor, her girls were a reminder of her bond with Leo.

Leonor dialed the phone number printed on the card that the man left on the table. She spoke into the voicemail, I cannot take that job. Here are my girls and I have to stay alive for them. Mercedes's was the next number she dialed. Leonor felt her life in Bogotá receding. She was moved to see Rosa lean forward and plant a kiss on Dahlia's forehead.

When Mercedes picked up the call, Leonor said, Mamá, estamos bien, llego pronto. Yes, very soon, within a few days.

CHAPTER EIGHTEEN

Leonor had forgotten about the Mocoa dust. Day after day, breeze lifted dust and debris, and laid it across the land, only to do the same the next morning. Dust, and plastic bottles and caps, plastic bags and cigarette stubs and splinters of glass, all accumulated on a miserable stubble of grass, or against the lone tree whose limbs grew over the fence that Mercedes had put up some fifteen years prior. When Mercedes had first arrived, she settled illegally here on an empty field, making sure to squat on as much land as she could. She foresaw the day when her children might need their own homes. So that not long after Leonor and the girls arrived in Mocoa, Mercedes partitioned a lot, and neighbors came together and gathered discards and remnants from construction sites, and hammered boards into walls and shingled a roof. They built a shed for Leonor and the girls. It was five or six feet in length and width, enough of a dwelling for a mattress and two chairs. An outhouse was on the other side. Nearing December, as expected that time of the year, there came the rain that lasted nearly a week until the skies wore out. The rain pierced the shed's rickety roof and turned the dirt floor to mud. By the end of the first week, the rain flooded streets and ditches, and the mud by the outhouse became treacherous. The rising river frightened Leonor. She no longer felt safe going there to wash her and the girl's clothes. Still, she went twice per week.

Using a rock as a washboard, she rubbed the blue detergent bar and scrubbed out the mud, and leaned down to lift the heavy bucket and pour the water. The motions of doing the wash were repetitive and gave Leonor time to think. She returned in the afternoons to the shed and hung the clean clothes on the laundry line strapped from the lone tree to her roof. She cooked rice, pasta or boiled potatoes for dinner on her one-burner gas stove. That she was living in a shed that brought to mind the family's homes in Puerto Guzman and Los Azules, that she often had little to keep her girls nourished, that she was husbandless and poor meant less once she put her energy into the chores of motherhood.

It was mid-2011. The time she had spent in Bogotá, Cali, Bucaramanga, and Pereira led her to take in everything with fresh eyes. She felt uneasy. She had evolved but her family and her immediate community remained the same in most ways.[1] Some of the neighbors and acquaintances—ones who offered friendship and hope—were former FARC. Later, some would rejoin FARC's dissident groups after the 2017 peace agreement. Those close to Leonor still divided time between Mocoa and FARC camps in nearby southern Colombia. Some neighbors and relatives worked as drug mules or were becoming big-time drug traffickers.

In Mocoa, a cycle of events she had endured was repeating itself because not much had changed and hardly anyone had left this place.

Leonor picked up her schooling where she had left off, and she finished tenth grade. It was what she assumed, from the ten years she had spent in the government program, that she was supposed to do. She still believed that if she studied, one day, someone would hire her and pay her a decent wage.

Walking familiar streets—reacquainting herself with her hometown, Leonor wondered, was Tico still alive? Did he still carry wads of cash? Did he still come now and then to Mocoa, and did he know that she had returned? Such thoughts became a daily habit like drinking coffee or washing dishes. Tico haunted her. She prepared herself for what she might say to him. It was a cruel joke that a lifetime ago when she passed the same street corners, her then-adolescent heart jumped with hope that he might suddenly appear.

There were days that Leonor could contemplate Tico's compassionate side. One day she said to me: "Of the thirteen of us who faced the war council that day, three of us lived. Because of Tico, I was not killed."

Since moving to Mocoa she had less access to government therapists, and I sensed I was becoming her sounding board.

Through army contacts, I tracked down Commander Tico's whereabouts. In 2015, he was captured by the army and charged with kidnapping and recruitment of children. He remained—at least until as late as 2017—in a high-security prison. He expected to receive immunity through proposed transitional laws passed as a result of the 2017 peace agreement. His case remained in limbo as far as January 2019. I did not tell Leonor, fearing it would cause her anguish.

Milton showed up three months after Leonor's arrival. He had resumed his trips out of town, but now he stood in Mercedes's doorway. His hair was thinner and his figure was rounded out. The sight of him twisted Leonor's heart—she knew what he was capable of. She wanted to find a solution to the threat that Milton represented. Wanted to find protection—a man, a boy-friend, a husband ... someone who by simply hanging around would dissuade Milton from hurting her.

Milton thrust a book on the table in front of her.

She recognized the author's name. It was the book by the reporter who had visited the group home in Bogotá on the evening that Rosa was conceived.

Milton explained the book was assigned reading in the high school nearby. Beyond angry, he struggled to utter words. He asked her why she had told people that he had sex with her. Why? His voice rose, his face was a red volcano. That I had sex with my sister?

Milton pointed at a passage in the book. That is not true, he said.

Leonor skimmed the text. Leonor was the first person featured in the book. (Though her name was not given—there was no denying it was Leonor.) The reporter described her hair styled in pig tails. Surely, her ramblings were those of an innocent girl, and that was her defense.

Leonor held the book close to her face to shield herself from Milton's wrath. Her hands trembled. She knew Milton had never touched her, though she always feared he would.

A wild and suffering expression came over Milton's face, and for an instant, Leonor felt sorry for him. Guilt settled on her chest.

The writer exaggerated the story, she said to him. It was as close to an apology as she would get.

Leonor could see that Milton was destroyed. She was well acquainted with that feeling. She knew the signs. His lips twittered. He jerked his ears in his fists. She turned her gaze away from him, as if to see what her girls might be doing in the next room.

The front door slammed behind him.

Maybe it was true as Mercedes had noted, that Milton was a shadow of his former self. Milton's wife had withstood his abuse. She lavished him with love and patience, and maybe Milton had grown sensitive. Could it be possible, Leonor wondered, that Milton was, after all, a gentle soul?

No, she decided later, some day Milton would kill her.

The puppy barked when anyone approached the shed. Throughout the night, when Leonor heard the barking, her hands reached for the girls' tiny bodies, relaxing only when she felt them, skin-on-skin. At least four times per night, she felt for and counted four limbs, ten fingers, ten toes, all safely beside her.

A week later, the puppy yapped when Milton showed up one afternoon. Milton yanked Leonor by the elbow, hoisting her close to him, face-to-face. He said, I am going to burn down your shed while you are sleeping. He had a look of intense hatred.

Leonor thought of asking her mother to talk to Milton, to beg him to tone down his aggression. But Mercedes had aged and she walked about with a cane. It was best not to worry her. Leonor was surprised that Mercedes's expression softened and her face glowed at the sight of her grand-daughters. Mercedes seemed another woman, truly. She was attentive to Leonor, genuinely happy to have her home. But the scar on Leonor's leg was a warning that Mercedes could lose her temper. Leonor recognized that if her girls were to have a kinder life than hers, she had to be a different kind of mother than Mercedes had been. Already, Rosa and Dahlia were beginning to fear Leonor's little eruptions.

It seemed to Leonor that she'd one day woken up a mom. On her body were bumps and the widened hips of childbirth. The responsibility for the girls lay heavily on her. But ever resilient, she made a home. Rosa, now four years old, brought home a lost puppy, and Leonor agreed to care for it. The puppy put a smile on their faces. From all the time spent in therapy, Leonor learned that if her girls formed fond memories of childhood, they might cope better as adults.

In Rosa, there was much of Leonor. Rosa practiced poses, smiles, frowns, and hand waving, all which also reminded Leonor of her father, the former paramilitary. Leonor still expected to feel anger toward Rosa's father, but of all that she had survived what transpired that night troubled her the least. Dahlia, too, was a version of Andres. Dahlia was kind, which meant she was sometimes seen as weak, and as Leonor understood Dahlia's character, she accepted that the heartbreak Andres caused her was not his intention. His loyalty had remained with his church and his parents and sister, and he'd been too spineless to form a life away from them.

Some days, Leonor wished to run away from her responsibilities to the girls.

"All mothers have those days," I said to her.

"No," she said. Her moods were darker. She wished to feel numb. Destructive thoughts crossed her mind. Where was the army major from the pension who had the drugs? She remembered Milton was likely to also have drugs, but she avoided him. In a daze, she walked the girls to and from school, the puppy leading the way.

But she scolded herself to be the mother she wanted to be. She cooked warm meals for the girls. She took pride that their clothes were clean.

"I would never kick my girls out of the house. No matter what," she said to me, referencing Mercedes, as if by habit. It was what she told herself, to keep her motor churning. *Do not be another Mercedes.*

Leonor carried on with a backwash of emotions. During this time, she posted photos on Facebook (at the local internet café and where I was able to call her and we could speak uninterrupted), and the images were of a tired woman, eyes filled with lament. Her mouth twisted into the frown that manifested the disenchantment she carried. Oftentimes, she walked around Mocoa—always the puppy at her heels—in a dreary state. Her gloom lasted days, sometimes weeks, in which she told herself that having returned to Mocoa meant she was a failure.

Some days, she fantasized she was among the well-heeled women she'd admired on Bogotá's streets. She consoled herself knowing that once, when she was with Andres, her closet contained dresses and high-heeled shoes. She had left them behind among the women in her last government home in Normandia neighborhood—and it felt like she gave up a piece of herself. "High heels are not for walking in the mud," she said, as a way of downplaying the gesture. Plus, in Mocoa such garments brought unwanted attention. She reverted to flip-flops and

T-shirts, and knowing full well how hurt she had been when Andres's family looked down on her, Leonor wildly revised her narrative—she told me Mocoa and its people were, indeed, as pitiful as Andres's sister and mother had pictured it.

Now and then, motherhood was interrupted when she walked to the hospital, shivery, sweaty with fever, as the genital warts re-festered. Other days, it was her leg, aching, swelling, causing her pain with each step. She was slimmer, as though she was being slowly erased. Before, life as the pretty girl had made her loud and giddy. Now, she exited the hospital and picked up her girls, and loaded with antibiotics, she was lethargic.

Good Friday of Holy Week meant Mocoa's annual parade. From blocks away, you heard the tempo of the guaracha drums, the tiple guitar and the accordion. It was a scene of devout Catholicism for the elders and booze for the youth. A woman was cloaked as a pregnant Virgin Mary, and she rode atop a donkey, led by a rope pulled by her Joseph. Locals lined the street where the procession passed. During the parade, a man followed Leonor. A newspaper was tucked under his arm. He shouted above the drums to get her attention. He asked if he could buy her a cup of coffee.

Leonor shook her head.

But this fellow—Segundo—arranged to bump into her during the next few days. Each time, he asked her out again until she relented.

The coffee shop was smoky and crowded. Leonor was mindful that drifting about were locals familiar with her life in the FARC. Still afraid FARC members might harm her because of all she had witnessed, she rarely ventured beyond a few streets where everyone was familiar.

She drank her coffee fast, scheming to get out of there. Segundo ordered her a second cup.

He told her he was once a paramilitary. He talked without hesitating, not fretting, even in the least bit, who might overhear. No one recoiled and no one lauded him.

His brown eyes combed her face for clues to how she was doing with this. She looked away. She sat back, flabbergasted. What was the motive behind his honesty?

He didn't ask about her background. Instead, he told her he now worked in construction.

The third time she saw him, when she was sure he would be okay with it, Leonor told him she was a "reinsertada" from the FARC.

I know, he said, unwrinkled by her candor.

Segundo, in his early thirties, frequented Mercedes's house, and he befriended the family. In a tone as if filing charges against her mother, Leonor told me that Mercedes fed Segundo and offered to wash his clothes. In turn, he fixed things around the house, electrical wires, some plumbing, moldy walls, and drafty windows, all without being asked. He lingered in the company of the family, and they expected him to be around. The twins, Sergio and Luis, high-fived him, and even Milton shook hands with him and asked him how he was doing. In Segundo's presence, Milton tamed his anger towards Leonor. Otherwise, her brother revived his threats to burn down her shed while she and the girls slept. In the darkness, terror kept Leonor roused and vigilant, any noise startling her.

Milton and Segundo, the two seemed a variation of one another. So it was that Leonor judged and feared Segundo for his past. She maintained a distance. When Segundo visited, she made herself busy with Rosa and Dahlia. She observed him from behind a door or from the other room—waiting to catch him in the wrong. Mercedes didn't give weight to her daughter's apprehensions.

Despite her mistrust, Leonor was flattered that Segundo made efforts to court her family. None of her past boyfriends had done that. Even Andres refused to visit Mocoa.

One day, Segundo volunteered to fix the leak on Leonor's roof. Outside, under a tree, his hand brushed against her shoulder. Next he traced her neck with his fingers. Leonor grew flushed, which surprised her. She was enthralled.

Ever the survivor, ever resourceful, Leonor surmised that in keeping Segundo around, he offered her protection from Milton. She asked him to move in with her and the girls.

Segundo reveled in other men flirting with her, standing too close to her, or pulling up a chair and buying her drinks, or offering her a discount at the grocery store. She would then comb her long hair forward, and flip it back with a flick of the head. She laughed rambunctiously and crossed her legs provocatively. Here was the girl I had known all this time. Like other men before, Leonor knew how to make Segundo feel she was the prize, and doing so awakened her energy for life.

She said, "He followed me around, all over town. Everywhere. He told me he loved me. I am not attracted to him." She dismissed that there might be true feelings between them.

Leonor, the former FARC, and Segundo, the former paramilitary, treaded along, mindful to not reveal details of their former selves. Their rule was to never watch the news together. And to never discuss politics. Outside the house, each kept their own friends and attended separate activities. He worked his construction job and she mothered the girls.

Weeks together turned to months. As they celebrated a first anniversary, Leonor settled with Segundo into a life engineered out of convenience. Eventually, they strolled through town, hands clasped. They embraced freely in public. ("In the face of the neighborhood, we appear to be the perfect couple," she said.)

They are in love. Those two are made for one another were what she imagined people said about them.

Segundo paid a part of the girls' schools, and Andres took care of the remaining balance. Segundo's presence brought her comfort.

From inside Mercedes's house emerged the commotion of the family gathered to celebrate Christmas. It was 2011. After Mercedes's sessions with the government therapist, she forced upon all her remaining children a new tradition to spend holidays together with her. Members of her family remained strangers to Leonor, and the reunions caused her anxiety.

Ligia, one of Leonor's older sisters, was already at the party, alongside her husband, the policeman. Weeks prior, Segundo had persuaded Leonor to come to a party at the policeman's home, and Leonor admitted the whole evening was not entirely bad. Her sister and brother-in-law acted hospitably. Yet, Leonor sensed that the policeman judged her, that when he saw her, he envisioned another setting, not so long ago, when the two might have been discharging bullets at each other. The scars from war remained.

At the Christmas party, Rosa, Dahlia, Mercedes's youngest boy, and the policeman's daughter chased each other around the house. To hear their giggles allowed Leonor to let down her guard. The innocence of their games was a reminder of the future and what mattered now. Pork roasted on the stove, and the air filled with the aroma of onions and cilantro. Buñuelos, fried dough balls, and natilla, custard, were laid out for dessert.

Milton treated Segundo with overt affection, and fetched him and Leonor each a bottled beer. It was as if Milton was a stranger she had never met.

Segundo often reminded her that long ago, Milton had done his best to shelter her from harm. Segundo said Milton would do anything to take care of the family. She did not tell Segundo about Milton's threats to burn down her house while she and the girls slept. Leonor knew full well that if incited, Milton would lose his temper. Nearby stood Milton's wife, and Leonor looked for signs of the abuse Milton had inflicted.

Some time that evening, in a corner, Milton and Sergio spoke in whispers. Leonor was curious, suspicious, to know why Sergio was holding on to Milton's every word. The brothers were chummy, almost giddy. Weeks prior, Sergio had posted a photo of himself on Facebook, glittery-eyed, both hands holding money up to his face, his lips kissing the cash. Leonor didn't know where he earned it.

Sergio was lankier than she remembered. He wore high-top running shoes, a sight that reminded her of Leo during the time when she worked for the señora in the market. Leo's high-tops had been a gift from Milton for having run errands for him. It saddened her to think what Sergio might be doing for Milton.

She approached her brothers with intentions to wish them happy holidays, but as she joined their circle, Milton and Sergio scattered. They vanished into the kitchen.

At dinner, the family sat around the table, in plastic patio chairs arranged to fit so that there was hardly any elbow room between them. Mercedes reminded them to express grateful-ness for the roasted pig on their plates.

Leonor was proud of her mother's strength, and wished to protect her mother. "Por fa," she said to me, "whatever you write, be kind to my mother."

Outside, the neighbors' firecrackers exploded. They were setting fire to an "año viejo," a figure of a man made from old clothing stuffed with hay and newspapers. It was tradition to make and burn such an effigy during the week between Christmas and New Year to release the hardships of the past and summon prosperity in the future.

Four months later, in April 2012, Leonor dropped out of the government program once and for all. She said the decision was well-thought-out. Still, it struck me, that it was perhaps a result of Segundo's influence. By the time Leonor quit, she was close to completing all the program's cycles. Only about twenty-five percent of former combatants who entered the program ended up completing as many phases as Leonor had.[2]

For a long time, she relied on the program to solve her problems. Now she resolved to not stray from a fruitful path, to stay positive. She wrote on her Facebook status, "Today, once and for all, I will allow life to continue without fear of anything, and I will live my life."

With Segundo, Leonor adapted better to the role of wife, though there were no formalities to celebrate or affirm their union. Every day, she walked to the river to fill buckets of water, which she hauled back. Once Segundo was home, she reheated the water in the stove for him to bathe outside, and she served him dinner. Once a week, when she stood on the shore of the river and scrubbed out the stains in the girls' clothes, he also did his load. She was grateful she had Segundo.

Still, she wanted a job and her own money. But it would cost her more than she could earn to hire someone to take care of Rosa and Dahlia when they were not in school. She half-joked that she might, after all these years, track down the men from the state intelligence office who'd offered her a lucrative job.

"You need to return to the government program and to keep your appointments with your therapist," I told her once.

"Why?" she asked. "You afraid that my monster will wake up?" Minutes prior, we'd combed over details of the night when she decked Andres while he slept and nearly choked Rosa.

She giggled. The next moment, she was solemn. She said, "The demobilization program was a fine time in my life. I look back and I thank God that I was able to receive that individual attention. But the program is not the same as it was. Now it's all a lie. The last time I saw a social worker was only once a month. All he cared about was a signature. He came just to get my signature so he could get paid. He didn't care how I was doing, how I lived, what I was thinking."

Another day, she said, "I want to get on television and tell everybody that peace is a lie. I want to tell people that they should not demobilize because the government won't help them."

Still, I suggested, again and again, that it was a good idea for her to have someone to talk to.

"No," she said. "It means leaving my girls for a few hours. I have no one I trust to take care of them."

Even though many former combatants had returned home to their families in Mocoa, the government therapists relocated their appointments to the next larger city, and she couldn't afford the bus fare to get there.

I had friended a psychologist in Bogotá who provided me with context to interpret Leonor's experiences. The psychologist worked for a non-profit, independent from the government, and I asked Leonor if I could give my friend her number.

"Yes, give her this cell number," she said, her voice cheering up, as though embracing the idea.

The psychologist called her, but it was difficult to truly help Leonor from afar.

CHAPTER NINETEEN

Once a month, Leonor and Segundo went out, the two of them, alone. It was a date. All month, they saved, to enjoy one sundae with two spoons, or to split a fruit salad or a pastry. They left Rosa and Dahlia with Mercedes. One afternoon, a few months after the Christmas party, they returned to find Mercedes in tears. Tears meant one thing, a death.

Mercedes could not bring herself to tell them. In the doorway, she trembled with her hands over her ears.

Rosa told them Sergio was dead. The army killed him, the little girl said.

Rosa was five years old but she did not shed tears. Possibly she didn't know what she was saying. Rosa put her arm around three-year-old Dahlia, shielding her.

Mercedes explained that Milton, Sergio, and others had kidnapped a woman in Mocoa. Sergio was assigned to guard the hostage. Hours earlier, the army had burst in, in a rescue attempt, and shot Sergio. Milton had plotted the kidnapping.

The evening of Sergio's death, Leonor found solace in her girls. Psalm Ninety-One: "He will call on me, and I will answer him; I will be with him in trouble, I will deliver him and honor him." She was accustomed to shelving her anxiety in Abuelita's teachings.

Sleeping between her and Segundo, the girls held hands. Dahlia giggled in her dreams.

Leonor asked Segundo if he had known about the kidnapping. He avoided her questions. Leonor also expressed unease in disclosing to me too much about Segundo. He was her live-in partner and when it concerned him, my questions were overstepping past her comfort. She and I could talk about most things in her life, but Segundo was off-bounds. The two or three times that he answered her phone when I called, he wasn't friendly. I suspected he wanted to hang up or tell me to stop calling. Perhaps he wanted to say her life, their life, was none of my business.

Before dawn a few days after Sergio's death, Segundo darted up from the bed, one leg in his trousers. He then hopped into the other leg, and half-way out the door, he zipped them up, and buttoned his shirt.

The puppy barked, and Leonor put a finger to her lips. She was concerned the noise would wake up the girls.

Segundo left the door open, and the puppy wandered out. Leonor spent most of the rest of the day wandering the streets, calling out for the puppy. It gave her something to do, something to focus on besides Sergio's death. She did not stop until she found the dog.

In the evening, Segundo returned, and Leonor warmed up his bathwater on the gas stove.

EPILOGUE

The municipal government in Mocoa paved some roads, put up traffic lights, and planted trees and lay grass in the main park. Leonor urged Rosa and Dahlia to take strolls with her, and the girls took turns leading the puppy on its leash. Leonor packed snacks, and for a few hours, they reveled in sunshine and fresh air. From the government's rehabilitation program, Leonor learned that her girls needed attention and someone to listen to them.

After what Leonor survived, she cherished seeing them growing up, and she poured her efforts into them. Leonor made sure they stayed in school and communicated with their teachers. She watched for signs of trouble as they aged, monitoring closely their comings and goings, as well as the company they kept.

Segundo offered Leonor protection from Milton and other men, and helped with the girls' expenses. Having him around also provided companionship, and so she was less likely to drink and do drugs. Leonor chose not to ask too much, or at the very least not to become emotionally entangled, with Segundo's dark dealings.

Time allowed Leonor to see that returning to Mocoa was not a failure, as she once thought. After having lived in different cities throughout Colombia, she accepted that in Mocoa—where almost everyone once had a connection to FARC—was where she could live without the stigma of having belonged to FARC. Elsewhere Rosa and Dahlia would be pointed out and rejected.

Leonor found some stability in her life. But peace in Colombia remained far away.

Every morning, I scanned the Colombian news portals, and I was sad to see the same headlines. Roads, electricity and water remained absent in the remote countryside. Coca production soared, even inside national parks. Despite the 2016 peace agreement, former FARC combatants regrouped and formed new drug trafficking groups. Displaced families poured into the main cities, not only from Colombia's countryside, but also from Venezuela, escaping the military dictatorship over there. Two former top FARC commanders crossed the border into Venezuela and resumed drug trafficking. One of them abandoned his seat in congress, which had been allotted to the group in the peace treaty.

Children continued to divide their time between towns and guerrilla camps in the mountains. The Colombian government's military again bombarded guerrilla camps to later find minors were among the victims. Impoverished mothers brought their virgin daughters to drug traffickers in exchange for payments.

The term "femicide" was thrown around by several think tanks. Women faced domestic abuse and sexual slavery, and their stories were hardly covered by local media. Women remained the silent victims.

The phantom La Llorona hadn't stopped weeping. People still spoke of her in whispers.

She drowned her children. Now she comes to abduct our children.

ACKNOWLEDGEMENTS

I began this book when I was twenty-seven years old, and I am now half a century old. I have many people to thank: first of all, Bertrand Delgado, my husband, who after twenty-two years is still my best friend. At Brown University, Virginia Krause first proposed the idea that I *might* be a writer. At Columbia University, Bill Berkeley, Anne Nelson and Mirta Ojito sent me out to cultivate sources and find stories. One spring day, Silvana Paternostro and I drank wine, and she spoke to me like a midwife, "You have a book about Colombia inside of you." At the New School, Jeff Allen believed I could shape my reporter's notebooks into a good read. Tom Jenks took a look at pages and pages of material, all in various stages, and he said, Let's get to work. Victoria Williams and I read many short stories together, and after each one, we said, "That was so good." Two grants from the Canada Council for the Arts gave me extra time to write and served as encouragement. Anna Ghosh, a kind friend and determined agent, always understood the fabric of this book. Along came Dale Peck and Evergreen Review Books, as well as John Oakes, Colin Robinson and OR Books, and they took a chance on *Leonor*.

Of course, I can see now that this all began when my grand-mother, Helena Aya, first passed on books to me, and when my mother patiently waited for me, while double-parked outside the Toronto Reference Library. Inside, I lost track of time in the company of books. I was thirteen years old. I also thank my father who has helped sustain my writer life since then. I have been gifted with a kind older brother who sometimes says he understands where his sister is coming from.

Most of all, I am grateful for Leonor's trust in me. It is my wish that she approves of how I told her story.

NOTES

INTRODUCTION

1   In a study done by a psychologist, under contract with the Ministry of Family Welfare, of the 86 participants in a halfway home for former child soldiers: 52 percent said they voluntarily joined the group because of their "like for the arms and the uniform." Cited in Defensoría del Pueblo, *Boletín No. 8, La Niñez y sus Derechos: Caracterización Psicosocial de Niños, Niñas y Adolescentes Desvinculados del Conflicto Armado* (Bogotá: Defensoria del Pueblo, 2002), http://www.defensoria.org.co/red/anexos/pdf/02/informe_9.pdf.

2   According to Sebastian Brett, *Colombia: You'll learn not to cry* (New York: Human Rights Watch, 2003), http://www.hrw.org/sites/default/files/reports/colombia0903.pdf.

    Brett wrote, "A commander's permission is required to have sex with a fellow guerrilla or to establish a more permanent relationship. Doing these things without authorization is a punishable offense."

    Further corroborated in Instituto Colombiano de Bienestar Familiar. "Lineamientos Técnico Administrativos de Acompañamiento Psicosocial." Draft Form.

3   Government psychologists summed up demobilizing and rehabilitating as "recognizing contexts, social, cultural and political, as

spaces and relations in which identity is constructed and decon-
structed, as well as beliefs and ideas of oneself and the world."

    Instituto Colombiano de Bienestar Familiar - Cecilia De La
Fuente de Lleras, Dirección de Protección, Subdirección de Restablecimiento de Derechos, *Ayuda de Memoria. Componente Psicosocial* (Bogotá: Instituto Colombiano de Bienestar Familiar).

4   https://www.ft.com/content/8ab52f2a-8c77-11e8-bf9e-8771d5404543.

CHAPTER 1

1   Found in http://www.insightcrime.org/news-briefs/farc-colombia-
stolen-land and http://www.eltiempo.com/archivo/documento/
CMS-12615401 and http://elcomercio.pe/mundo/latinoamer-
ica/fortuna-farc-guerrilla-tiene-finca-900-mil-hectareas-
noticia-1773560 .

    The Colombian press reported that an intercepted email
revealed the FARC's supreme head, Sureshot, accumulated fifty-
seven haciendas, valued at close to US$6 million dollars, which
his men took by force from small farmers. Found in http://www.
kienyke.com/historias/asi-estan-las-fincas-de-tirofijo-y-jojoy/.

2   Arturo Alape, *Las Vidas de Pedro Antonio Marín Manuel Marulanda
Vélez Tirofijo* (Santafé de Bogotá: Planeta, 1989), 43.

3   The moment that incited Sureshot to take up arms in the name of
protecting his close kin, as well as his character and life, is reconstructed from the extensive journalism of Arturo Alape, a registered Communist whose sympathy to the FARC gained him close
access to Sureshot. Arturo Alape, *Tirofijo: los sueños y las montañas.*
(Bogotá: Planeta, 1994) and *Las Vidas de Pedro Antonio Marín
Manuel Marulanda Vélez Tirofijo.* (Santafé de Bogotá: Planeta, 1989.)
Further corroborated by Victor G. Ricardo, High Commissioner for

Peace 1998–2000. (Bogotá, August 1999. New York, October 2000. London, August 2002. Bogotá, August 2005) Personal interview. (July and August 2012) Telephone interviews.

Further details in Carlos Arango Zuluaga, *Guerrillas FARC-EP: cronicas y testimonios de guerra* (Bogotá: Ediciones Anteo Ltd., 1984).

4   Electoral frauds and political persecutions described by Marino Jaramillo Echeverri in *Oposición y violencia en Colombia 1920–1934.* (Santa Fé de Bogotá: Ediciones Academica Colombiana de Jurisprudencia, 2003), 63–66.

5   Arturo Alape, *Las Vidas de Pedro Antonio Marín Manuel Marulanda Vélez Tirofijo* (Santafé de Bogotá: Planeta, 1989), 96, 105.

6   Ibid., 91.

7   Ibid., 49, 60.

8   Ibid., 105.

9   Ibid., 127.

10 Ibid.

11 Carlos Arango Zuluaga, *FARC 20 años: de Marquetalia a la Uribe* (Bogotá: Ediciones Aurora, 2015), 176.

12 Ibid., 177.

13 Details of life in Tolima department can be found in James D. Henderon, *When Colombia Bled: History of Violence in Colombia* (Alabama: University of Alabama Press, 1985), and Alonso Moncada Abello, *Un Aspecto de la Violencia* (Bogotá: Promotora Colombiana de Ediciones y Revistas, 1963).

14 Nick Miroff, "Colombia's war has displaced 7 million. With peace, will they go home?" *The Washington Post*, September 5, 2016, https://www.washingtonpost.com/world/the_americas/colombias-war-has-displaced-7-million-with-peace-will-they-go-home/2016/09/05/538df3c6-6eb8-11e6-993f-73c693a89820_story.html?noredirect=on&utm_term=.59ca0a871efc.

15 Jacobo Arenas, *Diario de la resistencia de Marquetalia* (Colombia: Abejo Mono, 1972), 56.

16 This chapter is reconstructed from James D. Henderson, *When Colombia Bled: History of Violence in Colombia* (Alabama: University of Alabama Press, 1985), Carlos Arango Zuluaga, *Guerrillas FARC-EP: cronicas y testimonios de guerra* (Bogotá: Ediciones Anteo Ltd., 1984), and Arturo Alape, *Las Vidas de Pedro Antonio Marín Manuel Marulanda Vélez Tirofijo* (Santafé de Bogotá: Planeta, 1989), 269–272, 284–357.

17 Scenes reconstructed from descriptions by Jacobo Arenas, FARC ideologue who survived the bombings in Marquetalia in Jacobo Arenas, *Diario de la resistencia de Marquetalia* (Colombia: Abejo Mono, 1972). Further details from Carlos Arango Zuluaga, *Guerrillas FARC- EP: cronicas y testimonios de guerra* (Bogotá: Ediciones Anteo Ltd., 1984).

18 Carlos Arango Zuluaga, *Guerrillas FARC-EP: cronicas y testimonios de Guerra* (Bogotá: Ediciones Anteo Ltd., 1984), 30.

19 Ibid.

20 Ibid., 29.

21 Described by Jacobo Arenas in *Diario de la resistencia de Marquetalia.* (Colombia: Abejo Mono, 1972), 27.

22 Carlos Arango Zuluag, *FARC Veinte años: De Marquetalia a la Uribe* (Santafé de Bogotá: Ediciones Aurora, 1984), 226.

23 Arturo Alape, *Las Vidas de Pedro Antonio Marín Manuel Marulanda Vélez Tirofijo.* (Santafé de Bogotá: Planeta, 1989), 337.

24 In 2001, about 59.8 percent of the Colombian population lived below the poverty line, and 10.28 percent lived in conditions of misery, according to National Department of Planning. In 2001, 59.8 percent of Colombia's children lived below the poverty line, and 9 percent lived in misery, according to the National Department of

Statistics. Cited in Defensoría del Pueblo, *Informe sobre los derechos humanos de la niñez en Colombia durante el año 2001* (Bogotá: Defensoria del Pueblo, 2001). Available online at http://www.defensoria.org.co/red/anexos/pdf/02/informe_5.pdf.

CHAPTER 2

1   Vera Grabe, *Razones de Vida.* (Bogotá, D.C.: Editorial Planeta Colombiana, S.A.: February 2001.)

2   Vera Grabe (Bogotá, July and August 2002) Personal interviews.

3   Further details in Laura Restrepo, *Historia de una traicion.* (Mexico: Claves Latinoamericanas, 1987), 28. Vera was part of the six M-19 commanders who participated in the peace dialogues (see p. 129).

4   Information in this chapter reconstructed from personal interviews with Vera Grabe (Bogotá, July and August 2002) and Nelly Diaz, former M-19 sympathizer and collaborator, and then Vera's personal assistant (July 2002). Further details from Vera Grabe, *Razones de Vida.* (Bogotá, D.C.: Editorial Planeta Colombiana, S.A.: February 2001.) Background information from Richard Gott, *Guerrilla Movements in Latin America* (London: Thomas Nelson and Sons, 1970), Ernesto Che Guevara, *Obras Escogidas 1957–1967.* (Havana: Editorial de Ciencias Sociales, 1985), and Fidel Castro, *Segunda Declaracion de la Habana* (Habana: Biblioteca Digital Ciudad Seva, 2010), http://www.ciudadseva.com/textos/otros/2declara.htm. See also Patricia Lara, *Siembra vientos y recogerás tempestades: la historia del M-19, sus protagonistas y sus destinos* (Bogotá, Planeta, 2002), Juan Antonio Pizarro, *Carlos Pizarro* (Colombia: Editorial Printer Latinoamericana Ltda. Lerner Ltda, 1992), and Laura Restrepo, *Historia de una traicion* (Mexico: Claves Latinoamericanas, 1987).

5   The environment of La Nacional University at that time was corrob-
     orated by María Eugenia Vásquez Perdomo, *Escrito para no morir:
     bitácora de una militancia* (Bogotá: Grafitto & Pizarra, 2011) and Juan
     Antonio Pizarro, *Carlos Pizarro* (Colombia: Editorial Printer Latino-
     americana Ltda. Lerner Ltda, 1992) 45.

6   Corroborated by Laura Restrepo, *Historia de una traicion.* (Mexico:
     Claves Latinoamericanas, 1987) 77.

7   Work of a revolutionary leader included much "explaining" to the
     masses, coordinating the movement of arms, and getting to know
     the areas, its people, and its routines, according to Ernesto Che
     Guevara, *Obras Escogidas 1957–1967.* (Havana: Editorial de Cien-
     cias Sociales, 1985), 39, 45. Vera's job in the countryside gave her
     the opportunity to carry out all this. Che Guevara, the hero of the
     Cuban revolution, believed the indoctrination in the countryside
     was the main goal which would lead to a triumph in the cities (56).
     Che Guevara believed women arose less suspicion, were better
     suited to win over strangers, and more apt to analyze and solve
     domestic issues (108–109, 120).

8   Corroborated by Arturo Alape, *Las Vidas de Pedro Antonio Marín
     Manuel Marulanda Vélez Tirofijo.* (Santafé de Bogotá: Planeta, 1989.)
     P. 69.

9   ANAPO background from Eduardo Pizarro Leongómez, *Las FARC
     (1949–1960) - De la Autodefensa a la combinación de todas las for-
     mas de lucha* (Bogotá: Tercer Mundo Editores, 1991), 42, 65–67, 73.
     Further background: César Augusto Ayala Diago, *Nacionalismo y
     Populismo: Anapo y el discurso politico de la oposición en Colom-
     bia: 1960 - 1966* (Santa Fé de Bogotá: Editorial Codice Ltda., 1995)
     and César Augusto Ayala Diago, *Resistencia y oposición al esta-
     blecimiento del Frente Nacional: los origenes de la Alianza Nacional
     Popular (ANAPO)* (Colombia: Colciencias, 1996) and Maria Eugenia

Rojas de Moreno, *Rojas Pinilla: Mi Padre* (Bogotá: Panamericana
Formas e Impresos, 2000).

10   Corroborated by Darío Villamizar, *Jaime Bateman: Biografía de un revolucionario* (Bogotá: Planeta, 2002), 289, 308. According to Villamizar,
     Bateman's relationship with Vera Grabe began at the end of 1975 and
     lasted eight years. Bateman did not make himself known to the rest of
     the M-19s though he was one of the M-19's ultimate leaders.

11   Details of the relationship between Jaime Bateman and Esmeralda
     Vargas found in Darío Villamizar, *Jaime Bateman: Biografía de un
     revolucionario* (Bogotá: Planeta, 2002), 209, 232, 250, 307, 338–339,
     354, 404, 429.

12   Jaime Bateman carried out urban intelligence and edited the FARC
     newspapers, *Resistencia*, and *Estrella Dorada*, according to Darío
     Villamizar, *Jaime Bateman: Biografía de un revolucionario* (Bogotá:
     Planeta, 2002), 209. Bateman defected from the FARC in 1972,
     according to Eduardo Pizarro Leongómez, *Las FARC (1949–1960) -
     De la Autodefensa a la combinación de todas las formas de lucha*
     (Bogotá: Tercer Mundo Editores, 1991), 32–33. Corroborated in
     Juan Antonio Pizarro, *Carlos Pizarro* (Colombia: Editorial Printer
     Latinoamericana Ltda. Lerner Ltda, 1992), 51–59.

13   "The revolution is a party!" said the Twig frequently; it was one of
     his favorite sayings, according to Laura Restrepo, *Historia de una
     traicion* (Mexico: Claves Latinoamericanas, 1987), 38. Corroborated
     in Juan Antonio Pizarro, *Carlos Pizarro* (Colombia: Editorial Printer
     Latinoamericana Ltda. Lerner Ltda, 1992), 193.

14   The M-19 ideology was influenced by Fidel Castro. They read and
     quoted Fidel Castro, *Segunda Declaracion de la Habana* (Habana:
     Biblioteca Digital Ciudad Seva, 2010). About women's role in revolution: 22–23. Available online at http://www.ciudadseva.com/textos/
     otros/2declara.htm.

Jaime Bateman's second daughter with Esmeralda was born in 1978, when he had already been with Vera for three years, according to Darío Villamizar, *Jaime Bateman: Biografía de un revolucionario* (Bogotá: Planeta, 2002), 338, 342. Bateman had many relationships with various women in the M-19.

15 Corroborated in Laura Restrepo, *Historia de una traicion* (Mexico: Claves Latinoamericanas, 1987), 21, 39.

16 Ideas from Fidel Castro *Segunda Declaracion de la Habana* (Habana: Biblioteca Digital Ciudad Seva, 2010), 34. Available online at http://www.ciudadseva.com/textos/otros/2declara.htm.

17 Famous phrase frequently repeated by Fidel Castro from *Segunda Declaracion de la Habana.*

CHAPTER 3

1 Daniel Jiménez and Eduardo Márquez, "La alegria del regreso a casa," *Cromos* (Bogotá: August 4, 1987).

2 Nelly Diaz, M-19 sympathizer and collaborator (Bogotá, July 2002) Personal interview.

CHAPTER 4

1 Corroborated by Natalia Springer, *Prisioneros Combatientes* (Santander: Corporacion Compromiso, 2010). Of the 437 former combatants, children and adolescents, boys and girls, in Springer's study: 66.1 percent had parents who worked the land, though very few said land was owned by them.

2 Corroborated by Natalia Springer, *Prisioneros Combatientes.* (Santander: Corporacion Compromiso, 2010). Of the 437 former combatants, children and adolescents, boys and girls, in Springer's

study: 59.6 percent of their mothers were housewives— but because of the need for money, 40.3 percent took on extra jobs. Of these, 21.4 percent worked land and 8.1 percent held a job in the commerce sector.

3   Corroborated by Radhika Coomaraswamy, *Integration of the human rights of women and the gender perspective: violence against women. Report of the Special Rapporteur on violence against women, its causes and consequences, Ms. Radhika Coomaraswamy, submitted with accordance with Commission on Human Rights resolution 2001/49, Mission to Colombia* (New York: United Nations Economic and Social Council: 11 March 2002). Coomaraswamy wrote, "Abortion is still a criminal offence in Colombia, punishable by from one to three years' imprisonment for both the woman seeking the abortion and the practitioner who performs it. The law provides for no exceptions, even in instances of rape, to save the life of the mother, or to avoid serious and permanent damage to her health. Abortion is the second cause of maternal mortality in Colombia according to Servicio Colombiano de Comunicación and Profamilia. The criminalization of abortion has a discriminatory effect on impoverished women: while women of higher socio-economic classes are able to obtain safe, though illegal, abortions, women with lower incomes are forced to seek dangerous backroom abortions. In addition, poor women are at a higher risk of pregnancy as a result of inadequate access to sex education and contraceptives. Although the social security system commits the Government to creating special informational programmes on reproductive health and family planning in less developed areas of the country, according to the information received from NGOs, these programmes were suspended in 1997. Observers point out that in abortion cases, opinions of the court are

often colored by Catholic religious arguments and cannot be said to be impartial." Available online at http://www.unhchr.ch/huridocda/ huridoca.nsf/70ef163b25b2333fc1256991004de370/5b35292ed4f-166d6c1256b67003aaec5/$FILE/G0211317.pdf.

4   In 2001, there were 69,681 reported cases of domestic violence, according to the Institute of Legal Medicine and Forensic Sciences. That translated to 10,981 cases of abuse of children, 41,320 cases of violence between couples, and 17,380 cases of abuse between other family members. Cited in Defensoría del Pueblo. *Informe sobre los derechos humanos de la niñez en Colombia durante el año 2001* (Bogotá: Defensoria del Pueblo, 2001). Available online at http:// www.defensoria.org.co/red/anexos/pdf/02/informe_5.pdf.

Corroborated by Sebastian Brett. *Colombia: You'll learn not to cry* (New York: Human Rights Watch, 2003). Available online at http://www.hrw.org/sites/default/files/reports/colombia0903.pdf. See also note 97.

5   Corroborated in Radhika Coomaraswamy, *Integration of the human rights of women and the gender perspective: violence against women. Report of the Special Rapporteur on violence against women, its causes and consequences, Ms. Radhika Coomaraswamy, submitted with accordance with Commission on Human Rights resolution 2001/49, Mission to Colombia* (New York: United Nations Economic and Social Council: 11 March 2002). Coomaraswamy wrote, "In Colombia, domestic violence is still considered to be a private matter. Consequently, incidents are underreported and it is not possible to determine the full extent of the problem. According to information received by IACHR, less than half of battered women seek assistance and only 9 per cent of them lodge a complaint with the authorities. Neither the State nor society is sufficiently sensitive to the need to tackle the problem of domestic violence. Impunity

for the perpetrators of acts of domestic violence against women is practically 100 per cent. Violence against women is part of the social context. Domestic violence is very common and, as in other countries, the level of violence escalates with the tension created by the ongoing internal conflict that impacts everyone's lives." In the hamlets where Leonor and her family lived in Putumayo department, there was no State authority present to denounce domestic abuse, even if Mercedes voluntarily wanted to.

6   Corroborated by Instituto Colombiano de Bienestar Familiar - Cecilia De La Fuente de Lleras, Dirección de Protección, Subdirección de Restablecimiento de Derechos. "Lineamientos Técnico Para El Programa Especializado y Modalidades Para La Atención a Niños, Niñas y Adolescentes Que Se Desvinculan De Groupos Armados Organizados Al Margen De La Ley" (Bogotá: Instituto Colombiano de Bienestar Familiar, 30 Diciembre, 2010).

CHAPTER 5

1   According to the academic Natalia Springer, of 437 former combatants, children and adolescents, boys and girls, in her study, 45.4 percent said had only "what is necessary to survive." Another 15.7 percent said they lived in a home where there was "insufficient even to survive." Springer concluded that 51.8 percent of the homes suffered of serious economic needs. Cited in Natalia Springer, *Prisioneros Combatientes* (Santander: Corporacion Compromiso, 2010).

2   Corroborated by Haidy Duque, founder and director, Taller de Vida, NGO for internally displaced (July 2002) Personal interview. "The work in isolated areas is with drugs. Even the dogs are thin," she told me.

Further corroborated by Natalia Springer, *Como corderos entre lobos: Del uso y reclutamiento de niñas, niños y adolescentes en el marco del conflicto armado y la criminalidad en Colombia* (Bogotá: Taller Digital Image Printing, 2012). Of the former combatants in her study: 79 percent lived in areas of cocaine crops, 44 percent were in areas where gasoline was sold illegally (gasoline is used for drug processing), and 43 percent reported presence of armed group near their home.

Also corroborated by Ximena Pachón C. *La Infancia Perdida en Colombia: Los Menores en la Guerra* (Bogotá: Universidad Nacional, 2009). Pachon reported international groups have denounced minors from bordering countries, Ecuador, Peru, and Brazil, cross the border into Colombia looking for work. They work as "raspachines," a term for those who pick coca leaves off the plant. Eventually they, too, are recruited into illegal armed groups. Picking coca leaves is one of the ways minors come across the guerrilla and eventually are lured into joining its ranks. Also corroborated by Carlos Alberto Plotter, FARC deserter and demobilized commander in the north-east department of Antioquia, in his testimony in US Congress. Cited in "Drugs and Thugs: A Status Report on Plan Colombia. Hearing of the House Government Reform Committee on the War" (Washington, D.C., 2004). Plotter told the hearing, "... mobility of the guerrilla which was essentially a mobile force. Now it's tied to the areas of narcotics production."

3   Found in http://www.unhcr.org/pages/49e492ad6.html.

CHAPTER 7

1   The use of minors to guard kidnapped hostages was corroborated by Sebastian Brett, *Colombia: You'll Learn Not to Cry* (New York: Human Rights Watch, 2003). Available online at http://www.hrw.org/sites/default/files/reports/colombia0903.pdf.

Further corroborated by Ximena Pachón C., *La Infancia Perdida en Colombia: Los Menores en la Guerra* (Bogotá: Universidad Nacional, 2009).

2   "Secuestrado Lorenzo Kling Mazuera," *El Espectador* (February 6, 1992). Corroborated by Jorge Miller, my brother's co-worker who witnessed my brother's kidnapping (August 2006). Telephone interview.

3   "El secuestro de Kling: sin pistas de autores," *El Tiempo* (February 7, 1992).

4   "Dramatico secuestro de un industrial en Bogotá," *El Tiempo* (February 6, 1992).

5   Corroborated by Sebastian Brett, *Colombia: You'll Learn Not to Cry*. Brett reported, "Several children who had guarded hostages said that they felt sad and upset about the captives' plight."

6   Found in http://www.cnn.com/SPECIALS/2000/colombia/story/reports/kidnapped/index.html.

7   Found in http://www.elespectador.com/noticias/infografia/40-anos-de-secuestro-colombia-articulo-459701.

8   Found in http://www.elespectador.com/noticias/infografia/40-anos-de-secuestro-colombia-articulo-459701.

CHAPTER 9

1   Corroborated by Sebastian Brett, *Colombia: You'll Learn Not To Cry*.

2   Corroborated by our family's bodyguard, a former counter-guerrilla soldier, who witnessed such torture during his time in the military. Moreover, according to Sebastian Brett of HRW, other forms of torture are cutting off fingers, pulling out nails, cutting off ears and nose, throwing hydrochloric acid on the face and body, burning the body with fire, and cutting open stomachs and removing intestines

with a knife while the victim is still alive. They also use a hot rod and place it throughout the victim's body. Cited in Sebastian Brett, *Colombia: You'll Learn Not To Cry.*

3   Radhika Coomaraswamy, *Integration of the human rights of women and the gender perspective: violence against women. Report of the Special Rapporteur on violence against women, its causes and consequences, Ms. Radhika Coomaraswamy, submitted with accordance with Commission on Human Rights resolution 2001/49, Mission to Colombia* (New York: United Nations Economic and Social Council: 11 March 2002). Coomaraswamy wrote, "Women are often killed after the rape and therefore are documented as a murder statistic only; there must be a move to document what happened to the victim prior to death by including information contained in the forensic reports in the official statistics, so a record is compiled of the various elements of the crime that is committed including the gender-based dimension."

4   Corroborated by Sebastian Brett, *Colombia: You'll Learn Not To Cry.*

5   Corroborated by Human Rights Watch, *Colombia: Beyond negotiation. International Humanitarian Law and its application to the conduct of the FARC-EP* (New York: Human Rights Watch, August, 2001), available online at http://www.hrw.org/reports/2001/farc/. The report stated, "The issue of intelligence gathering is particularly relevant to Colombia. Residents of territories where combatants are present necessarily come across information that could be of assistance to the parties to the conflict and they may, knowingly or unknowingly, transmit it, as occurs in Colombia. Yet the transmission of information does not in itself make such persons combatants. Among the pursuits that would not convert a civilian into a combatant are transmitting information that is gathered in the

course of normal activities or transmitting information that is not of direct use in launching an attack."

6   Corroborated in personal interviews with Beatriz Linares, Ombudswoman for Children and Adolescents (June 2001); Gladys Eugenia Zambrano, UNDP (June 2001); Alfredo Manrique, UNDP (July 2000).

Further, according to the academic Natalia Springer, of the 437 former combatants, children and adolescents, boys and girls, in her study: 24 percent said they were in areas with FARC presence, 9.7 percent in areas of paramilitary presence, 2.2 percent in areas of ELN presence, and 3 percent in areas with presence of another group. Of the survey group, 50 percent said more than one group operated in the area. Cited in Natalia Springer, Prisioneros Combatientes (Santander: Corporacion Compromiso, 2010). Further corroborated by Susana Villarán, Violence and discrimination against women in the armed conflict in Colombia (Washington, D.C.: General Secretariat of American States, 2006). Villarán reported, "Women can be direct or collateral victims of different forms of violence, as a result of their affective relationships as daughters, mothers, wives, partners or sisters" (17–18). "The sexual violence wounds the opposing faction in a special way because men are traditionally considered the protectors of the sexuality of women in their communities. Therefore, when the sexuality of women is abused and exploited, this aggression becomes an act of domination and power over men in the community or over the group under control" (18). Consuelo's murder may have "the objective of wounding, terrorizing and weakening the enemy to advance in the control over territories and economic resources," according to Villarán. Moreoover, Villarán also reported paramilitaries prohibit women from wearing suggestive or provocative clothing, and women who are seen as "free" become victims. She wrote, "... women's groups confirmed that when illegal groups occupy their territories, they decide how women must dress and to whom they can talk." Available at http://www.cidh.org/pdf%20files/InformeColombiaMujeres2006eng.pdf.

Moreover, Radhika Coomaraswamy from the UN also reported paramilitaries do not allow women to wear miniskirts, hipster jeans or tops which show their midriffs. Cited in Radhika Coomaraswamy, *Integration of the human rights of women and the gender perspective: violence against women. Report of the Special Rapporteur on violence against women, its causes and consequences, Ms. Radhika Coomaraswamy, submitted with accordance with Commission on Human Rights resolution 2001/49, Mission to Colombia* (New York: United Nations Economic and Social Council: 11 March 2002).

7   Corroborated by Public Advocate's Office, in Defensoría del Pueblo, *Informe sobre los derechos humanos de la niñez en Colombia durante el año 2001* (Bogotá: Defensoria del Pueblo, 2001.) Available online http://www.defensoria.org.co/red/anexos/pdf/02/informe_5.pdf.

8   Corroborated by Julián Aguirre, coordinator of the Ministry of Family Welfare's Program of Attention to Victims of Violence (June 2001) Personal interview.

CHAPTER 10

1   The FARC extended their dominion over land and drug trafficking following Pablo Escobar's death and the dismantlement of the Medellin and Cali cartels in 1993. See Rabassa and Chalk, *Colombian Labyrinth: The Synergy of Drugs and Insurgency and all Its Implications for Regional Stability*, 14.

2   Corroborated in http://www.mapinc.org/drugnews/v98.n661.a07.html.

3   Found in http://www.fiscalia.gov.co/colombia/noticias/acusacion-a-integrantes-de-las-farc-por-toma-de-miraflores-guaviare/.

4   Found in http://www.eltiempo.com/archivo/documento/MAM-739792.

5   Found in Andrés Pastrana, *La Palabra Bajo Fuego* (Bogotá: Editorial Planeta Colombiana, S.A., 2005), 83.

6   Robin Kirk, *More Terrible Than Death: Drugs, Violence, and America's War in Colombia* (New York.: PublicAffairs, 2003), 244.

7   Rabassa and Chalk, *Colombian Labyrinth: The Synergy of Drugs and Insurgency and all Its Implications for Regional Stability*, 19.

8   Found in http://articles.sun-sentinel.com/1998-08-06/news/9808050493_1_guerrillas-government-security-colombia.

9   Found in http://articles.sun-sentinel.com/1998-08-06/news/9808050493_1_guerrillas-government-security-colombia.

10 Found in http://web.stanford.edu/group/mappingmilitants/cgi-bin/groups/view/89.

11 Found in http://www.nytimes.com/1998/08/05/world/colombia-police-put-toll-in-rebel-attacks-at-200.html and http://articles.sun-sentinel.com/1998-08-06/news/9808050493_1_guerrillas-government-security-colombia.

12 For images of a battle, see Marco Duarte, "Fuertes combates del ejercito de Colombia contra las FARC-EP," YouTube, accessed July 5, 2013, http://www.youtube.com/watch?v=I4ap3E_iGmE.

    The FARC say they prefer to fight the counter-guerrilla soldiers who have chosen a career in the military, and not the young soldiers who are serving obligatory military service, according to Carlos Arango Zuluaga, *Guerrillas FARC-EP: cronicas y testimonios de guerra* (Bogotá: Ediciones Anteo Ltd., 1984), 44.

13 Corroborated by José Wilson, counter-guerrilla soldier (December 2001) Personal interview.

14   Sebastian Brett quoted a child describing a combat, "... That was
      when the International Red Cross helicopter arrived and found us.
      That saved our lives." Brett quoted another boy, "... She had a bullet
      in the stomach, but she was still alive. A soldier shot her dead,
      finished her off. Her name was Juanita. She was about eighteen."
      According to Brett, "International humanitarian law permits no such
      distinction: the summary execution of any captured combatant or
      civilian is a grave violation of international law." Cited in Sebastian
      Brett, *Colombia: You'll Learn Not To Cry.*

15   Brett reported paramilitary salaries ranged between US$366 to $488
      for three months. According to Brett, the paramilitaries call the
      army "cousins." Cited in Sebastian Brett, *Colombia: You'll Learn Not
      To Cry.*

        Further corroborated by Human Rights Watch. *Colombia's Killer
      Networks* (U.S.A: Human Rights Watch, 1996), available online at
      http://www.hrw.org/reports/1996/killertoc.htm.

        Moreover, corroborated by Radhika Coomaraswamy, *Integra-
      tion of the human rights of women and the gender perspective.*

16   According to Sebastian Brett, "International humanitarian law
      permits no such distinction: the summary execution of any captured
      combatant or civilian is a grave violation of international law." Brett
      quoted a child describing a combat, "... That was when the Interna-
      tional Red Cross helicopter arrived and found us. That saved our
      lives." Brett quoted another boy, "... She had a bullet in the stomach,
      but she was still alive. A soldier shot her dead, finished her off. Her
      name was Juanita. She was about eighteen." Cited in Sebastian Brett,
      Colombia: You'll Learn Not To Cry.

CHAPTER 11

1   In 2001, there were 2,700,000 children working and out of school,
     according to the Ministry of Labor. Of the number of working chil-
     dren, 1,700,000 were between the ages of 12 and 17, and 800,000
     were between 6 and 11 years old. Eight percent of all workers in the
     informal sector are children. Only 30 percent of working children
     attend school. Cited in Defensoría del Pueblo, *Informe sobre los
     derechos humanos de la niñez en Colombia durante el año 2001*
     (Bogotá: Defensoria del Pueblo, 2001), available online at http://
     www.defensoria.org.co/red/anexos/pdf/02/informe_5.pdf. See also
     note 84.

2   Of the 437 former combatants, children and adolescents, boys and
     girls, in Springer's study: 54.2 percent said they lived in an atypical
     family structure. Twenty-five percent said they not always lived with
     their family, and 25.1 percent said they changed homes at least once.
     Cited in Natalia Springer, *Prisioneros Combatientes* (Santander:
     Corporacion Compromiso, 2010).

          See also note 83.

3   The majority of former child soldiers in government rehabilitation
     programs have not gone to school past the third grade, according to
     Julián Aguirre, coordinator of the Ministry of Family Welfare's Pro-
     gram of Attention to Victims of Violence (Bogotá, June 2001–August
     2001, July 2002, August 2005) Personal interviews. Aguirre added, the
     rehabilitating children and teens mostly come from large rural fam-
     ilies and are forced to take up agricultural work at a very young age.
     More girls than boys reach middle school, and girls are often recruited
     for accounting or to operate their computer and radio systems.
     Women are who often handle the group's web sites.

According to Fabio Alejandro Mariño, a demobilized M-19 member and a consultant for Ministry of Education, about 39 percent of children in Colombia abandon school before middle school. (July 2002) Personal interview.

According to UNESCO, in 1999, there were 2,800,000 children not attending school in Colombia. That translated to 20 percent of the school-aged Colombian population. Moreover, in a study done by a psychologist, under contract with the Ministry of Family Welfare, of 86 former child soldiers living in a government half-way home: 8.14 percent attended school until 1st grade; 15.12 percent until 2nd grade ; 17.44 percent until 3rd grade; 9.30 percent until 4th grade; 18.6 percent until 5th grade; 12.79 percent until 6th grade; 8.14 percent until 7th grade; 3.49 percent until 9th grade; 1.16 percent until 10th grade; 1.16 percent until 11th grade. Twenty-five percent of the group said they abandoned school because they did not like school, and 25 percent said they abandoned school because they did not understand what they were being taught. Of the children in the study, 81 percent were in FARC; 16 percent in ELN; 2 percent in Ejército Popular de Liberación (EPL); and 1 percent in Ejército Revolucionario del Pueblo. Cited in Defensoría del Pueblo. *Informe sobre los derechos humanos de la niñez en Colombia durante el año 2001* (Bogotá: Defensoria del Pueblo, 2001), available online http://www.defensoria.org.co/red/anexos/pdf/02/informe_5.pdf.

Of the former child soldiers in a study by the academic Natalia Springer: 15 percent never attended school, and 84 percent had some basic schooling. Of these, 66 percent had completed first grade but were basically illiterate before joining the group. According to Springer's analysis, 37 percent of children abandoned school when they were recruited, while 54 percent worked before being recruited. Of those who abandoned school before recruitment, 31 percent said they were abused by teachers and/ or did not like school, 14 percent said school was too far away from their home. Cited in Natalia Springer, *Como corderos entre lobos: Del uso y reclutamiento de niñas, niños y adolescentes en el marco del conflicto armado y la criminalidad en Colombia* (Bogotá: Taller Digital Image Printing, 2012). Of 437 former combatants, children and adolescents, boys and girls, Springer found: 81.1 percent said they attended school at some point in their lives but "the majority" were illiterate. Many had worked and studied. Some reported the hunger and the difficulty to comprehend and assimilate what they were being taught. For many, school created a lack of self-esteem and self-image of low intellectual ability. Cited in Natalia Springer, *Prisioneros Combatientes* (Santander: Corporacion Compromiso, 2010).

4   In 2001, there were 13,352 medical reports that confirmed sexual abuse; 11,324 were of minors, according to the Institute of Legal Medicine and Forensic Sciences. Cited in Defensoría del Pueblo, *Informe sobre los derechos humanos de la niñez en Colombia durante el año 2001* (Bogotá: Defensoria del Pueblo, 2001), available online at http://www.defensoria.org.co/red/anexos/pdf/02/informe_5.pdf.

Corroborated by Radhika Coomaraswamy. She wrote, "Sexual violence in Colombia is also a matter of special concern. In 1995, the Institute of Legal Medicine of Colombia issued 11,970 opinions in investigations of sexual crimes nationwide. Of the victims, 88 per cent were women, for a rate of 34 women per 100,000 population. According to the information received, it is estimated that there are some 775 cases of rape of adolescents annually, and that the rate of rape for this age group is 3.5 per 1,000 women. Nonetheless, only 17 per cent of the victims denounce such acts. It should be noted that of all such attacks on women over 20 years of age, 47 per cent are by relatives." Cited in Coomaraswamy, Radhika. *Integration of the human rights of women and the gender perspective: violence against women.*

5   In 2000, 19 percent of Colombian women between 12 and 19 years old had an unwanted pregnancy, according to Profamilia, an NGO dedicated to women's sexual and reproductive health. Cited by Beatriz Linares, Ombudswoman for Children and Adolescents. (Bogotá, June, July and August 2001. July and August 2002) Personal interviews.

CHAPTER 12

1   Corroborated by Sebastian Brett, *Colombia: You'll Learn Not To Cry.* The information could include a photo of the person, personal data, and their address.

2   In a study done by a psychologist, under contract with the Ministry of Family Welfare, of 86 participants living in a halfway home for former child soldiers: 10 percent of the adolescents had left home much time before they joined the guerrilla. Cited Defensoría del Pueblo, *Boletín No. 8, La Niñez y sus Derechos: Caracterización Psicosocial de Niños, Niñas y Adolescentes Desvinculados del Conflicto Armado* (Bogotá: Defensoria del Pueblo, Nov. 8, 2002), available online at http://www.defensoria.org.co/red/anexos/pdf/02/informe_9.pdf. See note 61.

3   In a study done by a psychologist, under contract with the Ministry of Family Welfare, of 86 participants living in a half-way home for former child soldiers: 57 percent had worked before joining guerrilla; 30 percent of that 57 percent had worked processing coca leaves into powder cocaine. Cited in Defensoría del Pueblo. *Boletín No. 8, La Niñez y sus Derechos.* See note 60.

4   In 2001, 4,077 children were killed violently, according to the
     Institute of Legal Medicine and Forensic Sciences. That translated to
     11.1 violent deaths per day. Cited by Defensoría del Pueblo, *Informe
     sobre los derechos humanos de la niñez en Colombia durante el año
     2001.* (Bogotá: Defensoria del Pueblo, 2001), available online at
     http://www.defensoria.org.co/red/anexos/pdf/02/informe_5.pdf.

     Corroborated by Natalia Springer, *Como corderos entre lobos:
     Del uso y reclutamiento de niñas, niños y adolescentes en el marco
     del conflicto armado y la criminalidad en Colombia* (Bogotá: Taller
     Digital Image Printing, 2012). Additionally, see note 49.

CHAPTER 13

1   About 30 percent of former combatants lived in a war zone, 30
     percent joined the FARC because of poverty, and another 30 per-
     cent were victims of domestic abuse, according to Julián Aguirre,
     coordinator of the Ministry of Family Welfare's Program of Attention
     to Victims of Violence. Leonor fit all three categories. Corrobo-
     rated by Manuel Salazar, Consultant for Social Topics for President
     Andres Pastrana.

     In a study done by a psychologist, under contract with the
     Ministry of Family Welfare, of 86 participants living in a halfway
     home for former child soldiers: 83 percent came looking for the
     FARC to voluntarily join the group. Cited in Defensoría del Pueblo.
     Boletín No. 8.

     Natalia Springer, *Como corderos entre lobos: Del uso y reclutam-
     iento de niñas, niños y adolescentes en el marco del conflicto armado
     y la criminalidad en Colombia* (Bogotá: Taller Digital Image Printing,
     2012). According to Springer, of former child combatants in one of
     her studies: 82 percent had lacked access to water for more than a

year before joining; 99 percent lacked proper diet; 52 percent had
lower weight and height for their age; 98 percent suffered intense
and constant physical exhaustion. Of the group in her study, 81 percent "volunteered" to join an armed group, and 18 percent said they
were forced.

Corroborated by Graça Machel, *Machel Report on the Impact
of Armed Conflict on Children*. (New York: United Nations, August
26, 1996), available online at http://www.unicef.org/graca/a51-306_
en.pdf. Machel said, "In addition to being forcibly recruited, youth
also present themselves for service. It is misleading, however, to
consider this voluntary. While young people may appear to choose
military service, the choice is not exercised freely. They may be
driven by any of several forces, including cultural, social, economic
or political pressures."

Children come of their own free will, according to Sebastian
Brett, *Colombia: You'll Learn Not To Cry*.

Corroborated by Carlos Alberto Plotter, FARC deserter and
demobilized commander in the north-east department of Antioquia,
in testimony he gave in U.S. Congress: *Drugs and Thugs: A Status
Report on Plan Colombia. Hearing of the House Government Reform
Committee on the War* (Washington D.C., 2004). Plotter said, "At the
beginning it's a psychological pressure. You start telling the young
boys 'you're almost at the age of coming in, almost, pretty soon
you'll join us.' That's the beginning. There was what we would call a
national directive that arose lately and said that those in the guerrilla areas had - it was an obligation. They had to join up or else they
should leave. This is happening in the clandestine communist party,
and in the Bolivian militias." See also notes 8, 86, and 87.

2   According to Julián Aguirre, 90 percent of recruits to the FARC
came from rural areas, and 10 percent from urban. FARC have even

recruited street children in cities. "Anyone who can hold a rifle can be recruited," said Julián. However, the FARC have existed since 1964, and most child soldiers are born into the guerrilla. Their father, brother, or uncle are in FARC and they follow their relatives' path. Corroborated by Manuel Salazar, Consultant for Social Topics for President Andres Pastrana.

"My father came for me, I lived with my mother and my step-father, he murdered them and forced me to come with him," said a 16-year-old to a psychologist.

"A miliciano (urban member) came to talk to my mother and she packed my clothes and I had to go with them," said a 14-year-old to a psychologist.

"I liked the guerrilla because I saw that they were admired by people," said a 16-year-old to a psychologist.

Cited in Defensoría del Pueblo, *Boletín No. 8, La Niñez y sus Derechos.*

Corroborated by Natalia Springer, *Como corderos entre lobos: Del uso y reclutamiento de niñas, niños y adolescentes en el marco del conflicto armado y la criminalidad en Colombia.* (Bogotá: Taller Digital Image Printing, 2012.) In her study, 39 percent of recruits were contacted through their families, 33 percent were contacted directly, 9 percent were taken by a family member – which means 81 percent were approached by people they knew. Further, 39 percent said they had a family member in FARC. At first, the recruiter approached by sending the child or teen on an errand like transport food, deliver messages or make phone calls.

Further corroborated by Natalia Springer, *Prisioneros Combatientes.* (Santander: Corporacion Compromiso, 2010.) According to Springer, recruitment begins with contact in which the child or teen is evaluated and given a task. Of the 437 former combatants,

children and adolescents, boys and girls, in her study: 68 percent
"worked" for the group before formally joining. Of these, 52.2 percent transported mines and explosives, 9 percent carried out intelligence work, 3.8 percent were part of the urban militias, 12.5 percent
transported food; of the group, 89 percent reported having done
"favors" for the group. Springer added, "Voluntarily" also means a
"quota," or "contribution," or "tax," which is imposed on the family by
the illegal armed group. She reported, "To give a family member for
service in the ranks of the group is a common and systematic prac-
tice in these groups." Many children and adolescents in her study
expressed a desire to become part of a "larger project" to change
society. See also notes 8 and 85.

3   Corroborated by Jaime A. Carmona Parra and J. Felipe Tobón Hoyos,
     *Explanations for the phenomenon of female child soldiers in Antio-
     quia: A comparative analysis of the vision of girls detached from illegal
     armed groups and student children from the rural zones of Antioquia
     with a similar psychosocial profile* (Medellín: Fundación Universitaria
     Luís Amigó, January-December, 2007). According to Carmona Parra
     and Tobón Hoyos, girls are more likely to voluntarily join guerrilla
     groups due to poverty and domestic violence while boys are likely to
     voluntarily join to seek vengeance for the death of a family member,
     or for lust after a girl in the group.

     Corroborated by Natalia Springer, *Prisioneros Combatientes*
     (Santander: Corporacion Compromiso, 2010). Of the 437 former
     combatants, children and adolescents, boys and girls, in Spring-
     er's study: 6.5 percent said had they not joined the armed group, "I
     would be dead." Another 16.8 percent said "I would be worse off."
     This confirms that the decision of joining the group is based on
     survival for many. Of Springer's study, 23.8 percent looked for the

group by own means, as a way to escape imminent death; 75 percent were introduced or brought to the group by a third person: of which 26.2 percent considered was a "friend" who co-operated and sympathized with the group, and 20.1 percent came with an active uniformed member of the group. It's likely Redhead had contact with FARC and sympathized with them. Further corroborated by Natalia Springer, *Como corderos entre lobos: Del uso y reclutamiento de niñas, niños y adolescentes en el marco del conflicto armado y la criminalidad en Colombia* (Bogotá: Taller Digital Image Printing, 2012). Additionally, see note 85.

4   Only about 5 percent of child soldiers are indigenous, according to Julián Aguirre, coordinator of the Ministry of Family Welfare's Program of Attention to Victims of Violence (June 2001) Personal interview. Indigenous children move around easily in the jungle and are more likely to survive without needing the support of a group.

5   Such punishments were corroborated by Maria Perez, former Colombian child soldier, who spoke at the United Nations, June 2001.

6   Corroborated by Sebastian Brett, *Colombia: You'll Learn Not To Cry.* Brett wrote, "Besides IUDs, many girls described to Human Rights Watch being made to use Norplant contraceptive implants or contraceptive injections. Several mentioned getting birth control pills or condoms."

The use of a birth control injection and the presence of sexually transmitted diseases was further corroborated by Human Rights Watch. *Colombia: Beyond negotiation. International Humanitarian Law and its application to the conduct of the FARC-EP* (New York: Human Rights Watch, August, 2001), Available online at http://www.hrw.org/reports/2001/farc/. Further corroborated by Beatriz Linares,

Ombudswoman for Children and Adolescents (Bogotá, June 2001) Personal interview.

7   According to the office of Public Advocate, in a study done by a psychologist, under contract with the Ministry of Family Welfare, of the 86 participants living in a half-way home for former child soldiers: 13.3 percent said they were forced to use birth control. Birth control in the FARC is responsibility of women, they said. The use of condom is not norm, and there is great risk of STDs and spreading of HIV and AIDS. Cited in Defensoría del Pueblo *Boletín No. 8, La Niñez y sus Derechos.*

Corroborated in personal interviews with Beatriz Linares, Public Advocate for Children and Adolescents (June 2001); Julián Aguirre, coordinator of the Ministry of Family Welfare's Program of Attention to Victims of Violence (June 2001); Juan Carlos Restrepo, Founder and Director of NGO "Dear Soldier" (December 2001).

Further corroborated by Sebastian Brett, *Colombia: You'll Learn Not To Cry,* and Beatriz Linares, Ombudswoman for Children and Adolescents (Bogotá, June 2001) Personal interview.

8   Corroborated in personal interviews with Beatriz Linares, ombudswoman for Children and Adolescents (Bogotá, June, July, and August 2001; July and August 2002).

9   According to Beatriz Linares, Ombudswoman for Children and Adolescents. (Bogotá, June, July, and August 2001. July and August 2002) Personal interview.

10 According to Beatriz Linares, Ombudswoman for Children and Adolescents. (Bogotá, June, July and August 2001. July and August 2002) Personal interview. And according to the office of the Public Advocate, abortion was the third cause of hospital visits for all women in Colombia. Cited in Defensoría del Pueblo, *Informe sobre los derechos humanos de la niñez en Colombia durante el año 2001.*

(Bogotá: Defensoria del Pueblo, 2001), available online at http://www.defensoria.org.co/red/anexos/pdf/02/informe_5.pdf.

11   Corroborated by Sebastian Brett. *Colombia: You'll Learn Not To Cry.*

Further corroborated by Natalia Springer. Forty-two percent of girls in Springer's study considered it "an obligation to sexually attend to superiors" (48). This included touching and fingering (manoseo), undesired sexual activities, servitude, sharing girls between commanders, giving girls to other men as a favor. Cited in *Como corderos entre lobos.* See also note 96.

12   Corroborated in personal interviews with Beatriz Linares, ombudswoman for Children and Adolescents (Bogotá, June, July and August 2001. July and August 2002); and Julián Aguirre, coordinator of the Ministry of Family Welfare's Program of Attention to Victims of Violence (Bogotá, June 2001-August 2001, July 2002, August 2005).

According to report by Public Advocate's office, "These relationships may not be forced, but they take place in a context in which the girls are distinctly powerless, and the commanders may have life-or-death authority." Cited in Defensoría del Pueblo. *Boletín No. 8, La Niñez y sus Derechos.*

Natalia Springer reported, wrote, "it is policy of all illegal armed groups to violate the sexual and reproductive rights specially of girls and adolescents (forced sterilization, obligatory abortion or sexual humiliation as punishment), sexual servitude (the obligation to hold sexual relations with high commanders within the armed organization, or to participate in sexual activities against one's will), and the sexual use of boys, girls and adolescents to go after activities related to the group ('conquer or attract' combatants from other groups or public servants to extract information, promote recruitment, etc.)." Cited in *Como corderos entre lobos*, 8. Of the 437 former combatants, children and adolescents, boys and girls, in her study: 100 percent said to have had sexual relations; 54.2 percent said they initiated sexual activity between 4 and 13 years old, 32 percent between 14 and 15 years old, 13.9 percent between 16 and 18 years old. Further corroborated in Natalia Springer, *Prisioneros Combatientes.* (Santander: Corporacion Compromiso, 2010.); Susana Villarán, *Violence and discrimination against women in the armed conflict in Colombia.* (Washington, D.C.: General Secretariat of American States, 2006), and Radhika Coomaraswamy, *Integration of the human rights of women and the gender perspective: violence against women.* See also note 95.

13 In 2001, there were 1,553 reported cases of a mother's abuse toward her children; 2,164 reported cases of father's abuse; and 741 reported cases of stepfather's abuse, according to the Institute of Legal Medicine and Forensic Sciences. A 1998 study by the Ministry of Health found 361 children of every 1,000 are abused. However, they estimated a higher rate because few are reported to authorities. Cited in Defensoría del Pueblo, *Informe sobre los derechos humanos de la niñez en Colombia durante el año 2001* (Bogotá: Defensoria del Pueblo, 2001), available online at http://www.defensoria.org.co/red/anexos/pdf/02/informe_5.pdf.

In a study done by a psychologist, under contract with the Ministry of Family Welfare, 41 percent of 86 participants said they had been punished physically by adults in their homes: 74 percent were hit with a belt, 6 percent with a stick, and 6 percent with the adult's hand. Cited in Defensoría del Pueblo, *Boletín No. 8, La Niñez y sus Derechos.*

According to Natalia Springer, of the 437 former combatants, children and adolescents, boys and girls, in her study, 42.9 percent said they were victims of domestic abuse, 6.1 percent said they were sexually assaulted in their home, 8.6 percent lived in homes in which drug and alcohol abuse were common, 40.6 percent experienced serious economic problems that threatened the family's survival. In addition, many families lived in close proximity to activities of armed groups, and they could hear the attacks and explosions. Cited in Natalia Springer, *Prisioneros Combatientes* (Santander: Corporacion Compromiso, 2010).

Corroborated by Sebastian Brett, *Colombia: You'll Learn Not To Cry*. See also note 36.

14   Leonor joined the FARC voluntarily, in part, to feel accepted. Corroborated by Sebastian Brett, *Colombia: You'll Learn Not To Cry*. Brett reported, "The combination of protection and privileges provides a powerful incentive for girls to accede to, or even seek out, sexual relationships with male commanders." Given the possible advantages, young girls have sexual relations with them 'out of self-interest.'" Further, Natalia Springer reported, "On occasion, they are offered small recompenses, very useful in elevating their interest. The girls, for example, reported that they received new underwear, lotions for their skin and make-up, things they did not know of at home. In the case of boys, it is not the money but the respect and the visibility. 'One is nothing for nobody,' expressed one of the boys, happy to have abandoned his condition of invisibility the day he joined the de facto authority of the zone." Cited in Natalia Springer, *Como corderos entre lobos*, 35.

According to a report by the Office of the Public Advocate, 83 percent of adolescents in one transition home joined "voluntarily." Of these, 52 percent said they sought out the FARC for the feeling of power the uniform and the arm brought them. Girls principally look for a boyfriend with the uniform and the arm. Cited in Defensoría del Pueblo, *Informe sobre los derechos humanos de la niñez en Colombia durante el año 2001.*

15   Angel Rabasa and Peter Chalk, *Colombian Labyrinth: The Synergy of Drugs and Insurgency and Its Implications for Regional Stability* (Santa Monica, CA: RAND, 2001), 27, 64.

This group, deeply involved in the drug trade by the late 1990s, operated in the FARC's traditional strongholds in the departments of Putumayo, Caquetá, Huila, and part of Cauca.

Putumayo and Caquetá alone accounted for over one half of Colombia's coca acreage. In April 2000, three months prior to greater American involvement in Colombia, by way of Plan Colombia, there were 35,100 hectares of coca fields in Putumayo, and 28,000 hectares in Caquetá, out of a nationwide total of 122,500 hectares, according to the Colombian Armed Forces.

Also found in http://www.insightcrime.org/farc-peace/farc-criminal-activities-income.

16   Found in http://www.insightcrime.org/investigations/farc-and-drug-trade-siamese-twins.

17   Found in http://www.insightcrime.org/news-briefs/farc-earns-24-to-35-billion-drugs.

18   http://www.washingtonpost.com/sf/investigative/2013/12/21/covert-action-in-colombia/.

19   Corroborated by Sebastian Brett, *Colombia: You'll Learn Not To Cry.* Brett wrote, "Guns, powerful vehicles, and walkie-talkies are symbols of power. Many of the boys and girls considered guns to be 'bacano' (cool), and conversed about the merits of different weapons with the same casual familiarity that other children reserve for music or soccer."

20   Found in http://www.insightcrime.org/investigations/farc-and-drug-trade-siamese-twins.

21   In a study done by a psychologist, under contract with the Ministry of Family Welfare, of 86 participants living in a half-way home for

former child soldiers: 10 percent of the adolescents had left home much time before they joined the guerrilla. Cited in Defensoría del Pueblo, *Boletín No. 8, La Niñez y sus Derechos.*

22   Corroborated by Natalia Springer, *Prisioneros Combatientes* (Santander: Corporacion Compromiso, 2010). Of a sample of 437 former combatants, children and adolescents, boys and girls, in Springer's study: 100 percent said there was no possibility of leaving the group by individual decision or by group consensus. "The abandonment of the group is seen as the highest form of betrayal," Springer reported. Of her sample, 68.4 percent said they thought of escaping at least once, while 31.6 percent said they never thought of escaping. They all understood escaping was risking their lives as they were aware of war councils/ trials. According to Springer, the use of war councils/ trials for intimidation means high-ranked commanders understand abandoning group or running away or escaping is the will of the majority.

23   Corroborated by Sebastian Brett, *Colombia: You'll Learn Not To Cry.* Brett wrote, "Children are often required to do penance by making a public confession about their failings in front of the commanders and the assembled company. Others report being chained to trees for weeks, not allowed to speak or be spoken to."

24   Corroborated by Maria Perez, former Colombian child soldier, who spoke at the United Nations, June 2001; and by Public Advocate cited in Defensoría del Pueblo. *Boletín No. 8, La Niñez y sus Derechos,* 20–21.

Further corroborated by Sebastian Brett, *Colombia: You'll Learn Not To Cry.* Brett wrote, "Child combatants accused of these offenses are tried by a 'war council,' in which all the members of the company or front in question, other children included, have to participate. Children told us that the accused may name a fellow-combatant to defend them, while another is selected to lead the 'prosecution.' The procedure itself is conducted by several other members of the company. The defense pleads for clemency by asking for the accused combat- ant's service record to be considered. All present, bar the accused, may raise their hand for a chance to speak. Then a decision is made by a show of hands whether the accused should be executed or his or her life spared and a lesser punishment imposed."

Further corroborated by Human Rights Watch, *Colombia: Beyond negotiation. International Humanitarian Law and its application to the conduct of the FARC-EP* (New York: Human Rights Watch, August, 2001), available online at http://www.hrw.org/reports/2001/farc/colmfarc0801.pdf). The report stated, "The FARC-EP rarely informs accused persons of the charges against them or the procedure it intends to follow, and the accused are not permitted adequate means for their defense. Often, the accused are presumed guilty from the outset and they may not even be permitted to be present during the procedure. Finally, the FARC- EP offers no legal remedies to a decision, even in cases resulting in sentences of death. Such trials and executions constitute serious violations of the laws of war."

25 Corroborated by Human Rights Watch. *Colombia: Beyond negotiation. International Humanitarian Law and its application to the conduct of the FARC-E.* (New York: Human Rights Watch, August, 2001), available online http://www.hrw.org/reports/2001/farc/. The report stated, "The punishment for 'deserters' is the firing squad and this is applied regardless of the age of the deserter."

26 According to Human Rights Watch, child combatants accused in a FARC "war council" were told to name a fellow combatant to

defend them, while the rest of the group selected the "prosecution." The defense plead for clemency by asking for the accused's service record to be considered. All present, bar the accused, raised their hand for a chance to speak. I assumed that of anyone, Redhead, the trusted friend, might have risked speaking on her behalf. Then, per Human Rights Watch, a decision was made by a show of hands whether the accused should be executed or his or her life be spared and a lesser punishment imposed. Often, the accused were presumed guilty from the outset, and the mere initiation of the charges meant high-ranked commanders understood abandoning the group, or running away or escaping, was the will of the majority. A FARC "war council" offered no legal remedies, even in cases resulting in death sentences, which constituted serious violations of the laws of war. Found in Sebastian Brett *Colombia: You'll Learn Not To Cry.*

Further corroborated by Human Rights Watch, *Colombia: Beyond negotiation. International Humanitarian Law and its application to the conduct of the FARC-E* (New York: Human Rights Watch, August, 2001), avaailable online http://www.hrw.org/reports/2001/farc/colmfarc0801.pdf).

Further corroborated by Maria Perez, former Colombian child soldier, who spoke at the United Nations, June 2001; and by Public Advocate cited in Defensoría del Pueblo, *Boletín No. 8, La Niñez y sus Derechos.*

27 Corroborated by Sebastian Brett, *Colombia: You'll Learn Not To Cry.* Brett wrote, "Andrea, a sixteen-year-old, told us that her relationship with an older commander saved her from being killed when she was suspected of collaborating with the army. The commander, a high-level official in the FARC-EP's 71st front, had started a relationship with Andrea when he was thirty-five and she was twelve."

CHAPTER 14

1   Leonor's diet, lacking protein, iron and vitamins, increased the risk for any infection. See http://www.who.int/mediacentre/factsheets/fs375/en/ and http://www.who.int/leishmaniasis/resources/COLOM-BIA.pdf.

2   Found in http://talkingaboutcolombia.com/2015/05/04/videos-from-2014-show-farc-continue-training-minors-despite-peace-talks/.

3   Miscarriages are common, reported Natalia Springer in *Como corderos entre lobos.*

CHAPTER 15

1   Corroborated by Leon Valencia, former commander of Corriente Renovación Socialista, a dissident group of ELN, and current Director of Foundation Peace and Reconciliation (July 2002) Personal interview.

   Further corroborated in Instituto Colombiano de Bienestar Familiar. "Lineamientos Técnico Administrativos de Acompañamiento psicosocial." Draft Form.

2   http://www.eluniverso.com/2005/07/15/0001/14/03C8DD3E-A10B4D46B3E3CEF9EC6ADA38.html and http://www.caracol.com.co/noticias/actualidad/bicicletabomba-destruyo-refugio-de-ex-paramilitares-en-bogota/20050715/nota/187382.aspx[.

3   According to a report by the Public Advocate's office, "The most known psychological consequences of war are fear, aggressiveness, isolation, anxiety, insecurity, feelings of vengeance and desperation, and in more extreme cases psychosis and paranoia." Cited in Defensoría del Pueblo. *Boletín No. 8, La Niñez y sus Derechos,* 19.

4   According to the academic Natalia Springer, planting land mines is a job for children and teens because of the high rate of accidents and the need to safeguard seasoned adult combatants. Cited in Natalia Springer, *Como corderos entre lobos.*

     Further corroborated by Diana Roa. *Sembrando minas cosechando muerte* (Bogotá: Colombian Ministry, Canadian Embassy and UNICEF, 2002).

5   According to the Observatory of Human Rights of the Vice President of Colombia: there are about 70,000 planted land mines in 105 municipalities. There were 243 land mine victims in the first ten months of 2001; and 5,250 children from 1993 to 2001. Sixty percent of all victims are members of the Armed Forces and 40 percent are civilians. The FARC are responsible for 30 percent of the land mines. Moreover, according to a Sept. 2000 report by UNICEF, the Canadian Embassy and the Ministry of Communications, there were 100,000 land mines in 150 municipalities. This represented 20 percent of the entire country. Cited in Defensoría del Pueblo. *Informe sobre los derechos humanos de la niñez en Colombia durante el año 2001."*

     Further information in Diana Roa, *Sembrando minas cosechando muerte.*

6   According to the Observatory of Human Rights of the Vice President of Colombia.

7   According to Juan Manuel Urrutia, director of Ministry of Family Welfare, former child soldiers have had experiences that make them feel they can take care of themselves, and they often feel "stupid" going to school. In their world, they see no use for school. In this way, according to Urrutia, Leonor is different from the mold. (July 2001) Personal interview.

8   Corroborated in http://www.essex.ac.uk/armedcon/story_id/000760.pdf.

CHAPTER 16

1 Corroborated by Instituto Colombiano de Bienestar Familiar -
Cecilia De La Fuente de Lleras, Dirección de Protección, Subdirec-
ción de Restablecimiento de Derechos. "Lineamientos Técnico Para
El Programa Especializado y Modalidades Para La Atención a Niños,
Niñas y Adolescentes Que Se Desvinculan De Groupos Armados
Organizados Al Margen De La Ley." Bogotá: Instituto Colombiano
de Bienestar Familiar, 30 Diciembre, 2010.

2 Corroborated by Susana Villarán, *Violence and discrimination
against women in the armed conflict in Colombia*, 38.

3 Corroborated in Instituto Colombiano de Bienestar Familiar, "Lineamientos Técnico Administrativos de Acompañamiento Psicosocial."
Draft Form.

CHAPTER 17

1 While in the FARC, Leonor had grown accustomed to a different
self-image and a different ideal of femininity from what she was
encountering living in Bogotá's relatively conservative machista
society. It was difficult for her to adjust to being married to an Evangelical pastor.

Corroborated in Instituto Colombiano de Bienestar Familiar. "Lineamientos Técnico Administrativos de Acompañamiento
psicosocial" (Social workers' attempt to rebuild a new self-identity).
Draft Form.

"Overcoming Lost Childhoods." Found in http://www.essex.
ac.uk/armedcon/story_id/000760.pdf.

http://reliefweb.int/report/world/girl-child-soldiers-face-new-
battles-civilian-life.

2   "Overcoming Lost Childhoods." Found in http://www.essex.ac.uk/
    armedcon/story_id/000760.pdf.

3   Found in http://www.essex.ac.uk/armedcon/story_id/000760.pdf.
        Often, a former combatant's "life project" lacked adequate
    preparation, experience, skills and support, and so failed, confirmed
    a study by Y Care International. As was Leonor's circumstance, most
    ex-combatants did not have the formal education and maturity to
    establish and maintain a business.

4   Corroborated in Instituto Colombiano de Bienestar Familiar, "Line-
    amientos Técnico Administrativos de Acompañamiento Psicosocial."
    Draft Form.

5   Demobilized FARC provided intelligence that made operations
    against the FARC possible, and led to the killings of the top lead-
    ers.
        Found in MAJ Jon-Paul N. Maddaloni, U.S. Army, *An Analysis of
    the FARC in Colombia: Breaking the Frame of FM 3–24* (Fort Leaven-
    worth, Kansas: School of Advanced Military Studies United States
    Army Command and General Staff College, 2009). Found in http://
    www.cgsc.edu/sams/media/Monographs/MaddaloniJ-21MAY09.pdf.
        The CIA trained Colombian interrogators to more effectively
    question the demobilized FARC, and the CIA created databases to
    keep track of the debriefings so they could be searched and cross-
    referenced.
        Found in http://www.washingtonpost.com/sf/investiga-
    tive/2013/12/21/covert-action-in-colombia/.
        Former FARC offered valuable information about the group's
    chain of command, standard travel routes, camps, supply lines, drug
    and money sources, and voice intercepts, which often used code
    words. Sometimes, demobilized members were used to infiltrate

FARC camps to plant listening devices or beacons that emitted a GPS coordinate for smart bombs.

Found in http://www.washingtonpost.com/sf/investigative/2013/12/21/covert-action-in-colombia/.

In a historical twist, former FARC cooperated with CIA operatives, who were embedded in Plan Patriota and worked from the American Embassy. In turn, the FARC became aware that the government had much information and real-time intelligence on them. They stopped sleeping in the same place for more than two days in a row. They split up into smaller groups when traveling. Some in the leadership fled to Venezuela or Ecuador.

Found in http://www.coha.org/plan-patriota-what-700-million-in-us-cash-will-and-will-not-buy-you-in-colombia/.

CHAPTER 18

1   Corroborated by Documento Conpes 3673 de 2010, "Prevenir el Reclutamiento y Utilización de Niños, Niñas y Adolescentes es Asunto de Todos" (Bogotá: USAID, Vicepresidencia de la República de Colombia, OIM, September 20, 2011).

2   According to Ximena Pachón C. in *La Infancia Perdida en Colombia: Los Menores en la Guerra* (Bogotá: Universidad Nacional, 2009.) Available online at http://pdba.georgetown.edu/CLAS%20RESEARCH/Working%20Papers/WP15.pdf.

ABOUT THE AUTHOR

PAULA DELGADO-KLING holds degrees in comparative literature, French civilizations, international affairs, and creative writing from Brown, Columbia and the New School, respectively. This is her first book. It has been excerpted in *Narrative Magazine* (Winter 2008 issue), *The Literary Review* (Winter 2009 issue and reprinted in the 60th anniversary issue, fall 2017), *Pacifica Literary Review* (Winter 2017 issue), *The Grief Diaries* (February 2017 issue), and translated into Japanese for happano.org (January 2017 issue). For this book, she received two grants from the Canada Council for the Arts, and won the OneWorld Prize in nonfiction from the Pan African Literary Forum, for which she was awarded a trip to Accra, Ghana to share her work.

Paula's website is www.pauladelgadokling.com. Her reportage, "El Diario de Maher Arar," was anthologized in *Las Mejores Crónicas de Gatopardo* (Random House Mondadori, 2006). Since March 2005, she has been an assistant editor at *Narrative Magazine*. She lives in New York.